Hugh Farmer, William Worthington

Letters to the Rev. Dr. Worthington

in answer to his late publication, intitled An impartial enquiry into the case of the

gospel demoniaks

Hugh Farmer, William Worthington

Letters to the Rev. Dr. Worthington
in answer to his late publication, intitled An impartial enquiry into the case of the gospel demoniaks

ISBN/EAN: 9783337284671

Printed in Europe, USA, Canada, Australia, Japan

Cover: Foto ©Lupo / pixelio.de

More available books at **www.hansebooks.com**

TO THE

Rev. DR. WORTHINGTON,

In Answer to his late Publication,

INTITLED,

An IMPARTIAL ENQUIRY into the Case of the GOSPEL DEMONIACKS.

By HUGH FARMER.

The notions which we receive from our senses, often render it proper, if not necessary, that matters should be expressed according to the system of appearances; as is the general practice at present, though we live in a philosophical age; the popular language being always the best understood, and therefore the most proper concerning subjects incidentally mentioned, and not professedly treated of.

Dr. Worthington's Introduction to The Scripture-Theory of the Earth, p. 7.

LONDON:

Printed for J. BUCKLAND and G. ROBINSON, in Pater-noster Row, 1778.

CONTENTS.

LETTER I.

ON Dr. *Worthington's treatment of the advocates for the antidemoniac system*, p. 1.

LETTER II.

On Dr. *W's notion of possessing demons*, p. 24. *An examination of his arguments in support of that notion taken:* I. *From the writings of the Heathens*, p. 27. II. *From the writings of the Jews*, p. 41. III. *From the language of Christ and his apostles*, p. 47. IV. *From the sentiments of the primitive Christians*, p. 64. *The importance of determining the opinion of the ancients concerning possessing demons*, p. 76. *The moral character of these demons*, p. 77. *A denial that possessions were referred to the devil, does not infer a denial of his existence, much less of the existence of human spirits*, p. 81.

LETTER III.

On Dr. W's account of the nature of demoniacal possessions, p. 87. *The true notion of them stated, p.* 98. *Why possessions are distinguished from bodily diseases, and from lunacies, p.* 105.

LETTER IV.

On Dr. W's proofs of the reality of demoniacal possessions, p. 110. *His principal argument, viz. that taken from possessions and dispossessions being attested as facts in the New Testament, stated, ib. In answer to this argument, it is shewn:* I. *That the possessions and dispossessions of demons, (as explained by Dr. W.) even supposing them to be real facts, are not in their own nature objects of sense; and therefore can not be supported by the testimony of sense, p.* 114. II. *That the reality of possessions and dispossessions neither was, nor could fitly be, established by the authority of Christ and his apostles, considered as inspired and infallible persons, p.* 123. III. *That the language of the*

CONTENTS.

the New Testament relative to possessions, did always imply certain outward and sensible symptoms and effects, or the disorder and cure of demoniacs, p. 128; *that this language was used principally to express those symptoms and effects, p.* 129; *and commonly without any other intention, p.* 144; *and that it must have been so used by the evangelists, p.* 148. *A distinct examination of the several modes of speech used by Christ and his apostles in curing demoniacs, and describing their case, p.* 129—144. *Peculiar reasons for believing that possessions in the New Testament denote only madness, without any reference to the cause from which it might proceed, p.* 148. *It is shewn farther;* IV. *That the evangelists might describe the disorder and cure of demoniacs by possessions and dispossessions, without making themselves answerable for the hypothesis on which this language was originally founded, p.* 154. *Three reasons for this assigned.* 1. *The universal custom of speaking on many subjects in the popular language, though admitted to have been originally grounded on a false philosophy, p.* 154. 2. *The certain conformity*

of

of the sacred writers to this custom, on many occasions; and particularly when they assert the immobility of the earth, and the motion of the sun, the denial of which was once deemed a most impious heresy, p. 155. *What may be urged in vindication of the sacred writers in this respect*, p. 160. *There is no peculiar reason for their not describing the case of the demoniacs in the vulgar language*, p. 164, *note* (ª). 3. *Their speaking of demons and bodily disorders in mere conformity to the vulgar opinion concerning them, without giving their sanction to it, is a farther proof that they might do the same on the subject of demoniacal possession*, p. 165. *Hence it follows, that the possessions and dispossessions spoken of in the New Testament, though real facts are not attested as such in the sense explained by Dr. W.* p. 168, *and that there is no colour to charge the author of the Essay with maintaining, that it is lawful to profess one thing, and believe the contrary*, p. 170; *or with impeaching the character and credit of Christ and his apostles*, p. 171, *or with abusing the Scriptures*, p. 174, *or with supposing that Christ countenanced superstition*, p. 175.

LETTER

LETTER V.

On Dr. W's farther proofs of the reality of possessions, drawn from the history of the New Testament demoniacs, p. 177. *His arguments from the silence of the Sadducees, and of Herod,* ib. *from the objection of the Pharisees, that Christ cast out demons by Beelzebub, p.* 178, *from Christ's refutation of this objection, p.* 179; *from some circumstances in the case of particular demoniacs, p.* 181, *such as their uncommon strength, and their knowledge of Jesus as the Messiah,* ib. *Several observations on Dr. W's account of the Gadarene demoniac, p.* 183. *His false account of Simon Magus, p.* 193.

LETTER VI.

On the proof of demoniacal possession, 1. *From Reason, p.* 197. 2. *From Experience, p.* 202. 3. *From Tradition, p.* 208. 4. *From Revelation, p.* 214. *That the anti-demoniac system does no prejudice to revelation, p.* 215. *That the vulgar hypothesis has*

has not a single recommendation, p. 216; that, besides exposing the miracles described by the dispossessions of demons to contempt, p. 218: 1. It subverts the fundamental principle of all true religion, the sole dominion of *Jehovah* over the course of nature, p. 219. 2. It contradicts the Scripture doctrine concerning the demons or gods of the *Heathens*, p. 221. 3. It destroys the evidence of revelation, or the force of those miracles which were wrought to attest it's divine original, p. 229. 4. It casts the greatest reflection on the character and conduct of *Christ* and his apostles, p. 231. Recapitulation, p. 235. Conclusion, p. 238.

ADVERTISEMENT of the PRINTER.

BY *Inquiry*, and *Inq.* in the following sheets, is meant, Dr. Worthington's Inquiry into the Case of the Gospel Demoniacs,

And by *Essay* is meant, Mr. Farmer's Essay on the Demoniacs of the New Testament.

LETTER I.

Tuesday, Nov. 25, 1777.

Reverend Sir,

WHEN I first heard of your *Impartial Inquiry into the Case of the Gospel Demoniacs*, I expected to see the subject handled to advantage: for though I had never read any of your writings, I was no stranger to your reputation. It was natural for me, therefore, to conclude, that your learning would enable you to throw new light upon your subject; and your benevolence and candour prevent you from exceeding the bounds of moderation, in your treatment of those who differ from you in opinion. I recollected with pleasure, the following citation from your book upon *Redemption*, in a work of the very learned and worthy Bishop of Carlisle; viz. *I think it may be said, in honour of the present*

present age, that controversy is carried on with more DECENCY *and* GOOD MANNERS, *than in any former period of time that can be named*[a].

With these prejudices in your favour, I sat down to the perusal of your late publication; and I heartily wish that my expectations had been answered: but I cannot feel the force of your reasoning, much less can I applaud the temper and spirit you discover. Throughout the whole of your performance, you have misrepresented my sentiments, (through inattention, I hope, rather than design) and supplied the defect of argument with an uncommon measure of abuse.

I acknowledge, however, that you have paid considerable attention to your subject, and have offered some things upon it that may deserve to be considered. At the same time I am sensible that your rank and character can scarce fail of recommending your

[a] *Law*'s Considerations, p. 244, 5th edit. in the notes. The passage is taken from Dr. Worthington's *Essay on Redemption*, p. 136, 2d edit.

work

work to the attention of the public. To the public, therefore, and to you, Sir, it might seem disrespectful, not to assign the reasons of my still adhering to that hypothesis which you so severely condemn. Nor am I altogether without hope, that by reducing the argument of my *Essay on the Demoniacs of the New Testament* within a narrow compass, by shewing it in different lights, and especially by confirming it by some additional observations, I may possibly lessen even Dr. Worthington's prejudices against it; or, at least, convince others, that it is better supported than he is willing to allow.

Before I undertake to examine your *reasonings* against the *Essay*, it will be necessary to take notice of your *censures* of its author, and of all those in general who maintain the same sentiments with him. These censures, indeed, may seem foreign from the subject in dispute; but you introduce them so frequently, and manage them with such address, that were they totally overlooked, they might have an undue

undue influence on those who are least capable of judging of the merits of the controversy between us, and of determining on whose side the truth is to be found. And while I am attempting to efface the ill impression which possibly some weak minds may have received from your false accusations, many observations will be made relative to our main subject.

It cannot have escaped your observation, Sir, that scarce has any prejudice a greater influence in perverting the judgment, than that arising from *the character* of the persons who espouse the doctrines proposed to our belief. The veneration that men have for their parents and tutors, for writers of great name and eminent piety, inclines them to adopt all their opinions at once, without examination. On the other hand, they reject, without hesitation, the doctrines proposed to them by those who are censured as impious and prophane. Fearing to partake of other men's guilt, they dread conviction as a crime. Hence it is, that controversial writers, instead of answering

the

the arguments of their opponents, too often strive to render their persons odious by misrepresentation and calumny. But, is it possible that Dr. Worthington should stoop to these arts of controversy? Let facts determine the question.

With what other view than that of creating prejudices against those who differ from you on the subject of your *Inquiry*, could you give the following account of them in general? *The divinity of the Holy Ghost, and even his personality, is denied, I do not say by this writer, but by others of his principles*[b]. It might be putting you to great difficulties to require from you a proof of what you assert; and, at the same time, would be wandering far from our subject. Most certainly, no one can possibly infer, either from men's denial, or from their belief, of demoniacal possessions, what sentiments they entertain concerning the personality and divinity of the Holy Ghost.

[b] Inquiry, p. 70.

You advance farther, and say,[c] *It should be seriously considered, whether the speaking of a word against Christ's casting out devils by the Spirit of God, be not speaking against him, and that divine Spirit too.* In order to convey into the minds of your readers the very worst impression of your opponents, you here insinuate, with an air of great seriousness, that they may be chargeable with the heinous guilt of blasphemy against the Holy Ghost. On what do you ground this suspicion? Why, it seems, they deny (in your opinion) the fact, that Christ did cast out demons, and thereby virtually deny the power by which he did perform it[d]. You well know, that all Christians are agreed in referring the miracle described by *casting out demons* (whatever be the import of that expression) to the Spirit of God; and that the dispute between them respects merely the *nature*, not the *author* of the miracle. Of blasphemy against the Holy Ghost, therefore, none of them can be guilty, according to your own account of

[c] Inquiry, p. 71.   [d] Inq. p. 68.

it;

it: for you say, it consisted *in ascribing the works of God to the devil*[e]. Nay, you affirm, *that there is no one in these days that can be so impious, as to attribute the works of God to the devil*[f]. Your opponents, therefore, if they are guilty of blasphemy against the Holy Ghost, are *more* impious than any one in these days *can* be! It would have sounded more like truth, if you had been content with saying, as surely you well might, that they were only as impious as men could *possibly* be, or were in great danger of becoming so. As a friend, permit me to advise you never to let your calumnies bear upon themselves their own confutation; which they are sure to do, when they exceed the limits of possibility. If you only say of those who differ from you, that they *will dispute the plainest things in the world*[g]; that they are *hardened against conviction*[h]; that they are *iniquitous and perverse*[i]; and that their *opinions are such as argue the height of impiety to conceive*[k]: all

[e] Inquiry, p. 67. [f] Inq. p. 71. [g] Inq. p. 63.
[h] p. 41. See p. 75 [i] p. 117. [k] p. 132.

this may pass with those who take every thing upon trust. But don't insinuate, that they are *more* impious than any man *can* be, lest it should hurt your own credit. Begging you to excuse this freedom, I proceed to observe that

You give us this farther account of those who differ from you: *Nor was there any doubt amongst them* (the Heathens in general, the ancient Jews, and the primitive Christians) *in this respect* (in respect to the existence of demons, and the reality of their possessions), *unless it was amongst such as were of atheistical or libertine principles*[h]. You add, *Pomponatius, Vaninus, Hobbes, Spinosa, and Bekker, who, it hath been observed, have patronized the opinion, that possessions were nothing more than natural diseases, are all well known to have been profane and atheistical writers.* There is no crime in agreeing with atheists in any innocent opinion. That under our present consideration, has no relation to atheism. Nor is it true, that

[h] Inquiry, p. 214.   [i] Inq p. 214, 215.

atheists

atheifts do patronize this opinion; they rather take occafion from the oppofite one, to fortify themfelves in their irreligion; not being able to reconcile it with the wifdom and goodnefs of God, and with the order of nature. It is the genuine theift alone, that from an earneft defire of vindicating the ways of God to man, is folicitous to fhew, that reputed poffeffions are natural difeafes. The famous Bekker undertook the defence of this opinion; but he was not, what you falfely reprefent him, a perfon *well known to have been a profane and atheiftical writer*; but, on the contrary, one who was well known to have been a moft ferious Chriftian, whofe general principles were what even you efteem orthodox. He was a man of admirable parts and learning, a moft indefatigable inquirer after truth, bold and fteadfaft in maintaining what to him appeared as fuch, at the hazard of every worldly intereft. His enemies, who, through envy, malice and bigotry, fufpended him from the holy communion, and depofed him from the office of a minifter,

nifter, never raifed a fingle objection againft his morals*.

But you infift upon it, that the anti-demoniac fyftem *is patronized chiefly by fuch, among antients and moderns, as are a difgrace to any caufe*ᵏ. Can you review this language with fatisfaction, when you recollect that the chief patrons of the fyftem you

---

* I do not bear this teftimony to Bekker, becaufe I approve all his opinions (for to me many of them appear erroneous), but for the fake of doing juftice to his injured memory. Let not thofe who, under the bias of education, have adopted popular opinions, be forward to difparage men of the moft diftinguifhed abilities; who, from an ardent and unbiaffed love of truth, fpared no pains to difcover it, and were willing to fuffer difgrace and the fevereft perfecution, rather than act contrary to their conviction. However miftaken on fome points they might be, yet their talents, and efpecially their exalted virtues, entitle them to the higheft veneration of mankind. It is with equal injuftice that you brand Pomponatius as an atheift. His diftinguifhing opinion concerning the human foul has been adopted by fome of the moft refpectable perfons in the Chriftian church. It is unbecoming a perfon of your learning and liberality to deal in groundlefs fcandal.

ᵏ Inquiry, p. 223.

condemn,

condemn, are defervedly ranked amongft the brighteft ornaments of human nature[l]? Is it without reafon that Ariftotle has been ftiled the prince of the philofophers? Can you name a man in the whole heathen world fuperior to Hippocrates, for foundnefs of judgment or fincere piety? Whom amongft his opponents will you weigh in the fcales againft Jofeph Mede? Scarce is his equal any where to be found in compafs of theological learning, or in depth of penetration. Great names have lately appeared in defence of his opinion; his illuftrious kinfman, Dr. Richard Mead, the learned Dr. Sykes, Dr. Arthur Young, Dr. Lardner[m]. Thefe, Sir, are the chief patrons of this opinion; and will you fay, that they are a difgrace to any caufe? Retract your cenfure, if not for the fake of the moderns, yet at leaft to fave the credit of the ancients (of which you are fo jealous); for fome even of the Fathers, though in their popular difcourfes they afferted the reality

[l] See Effay, p. 155.
[m] See alfo Dr. Douglas's Criterion, p. 263, note, and Boyle's Lect. fol. ed. v. 3. p. 265.

of possessions, yet did not firmly believe it. St. Austin says, "perhaps he who in truth was mad, was on that account *thought* to be possessed[l]. Jerome, Theodoret, Cyril, Theophylact, Cæsarius, and many other ancients often use the same, or very similar language, with the orthodox Bishop of Hippo[m].

If you were capable of abusing the chief patrons of the antidemoniac hypothesis, I may well forgive your virulence against the most inconsiderable advocate for it. The picture you have drawn of me is not a very flattering one; the reader shall judge what likeness it bears to the original. You would persuade the world, that *I condemn scripture doctrines in the lump, and over-rule the Scipture itself, in a decretorial manner*[n]; because I do not submit to your explications of Scripture. If Rousseau is offended at the supposition, that Christ wanted to learn

[l] Forte *revera phreneticus* erat, sed propter ista dæmonium pati *putabatur*. Augustin. de *Genesi* ad litter. xii. 17.

[m] Introduction to Essay, p. 7, note (e); and Essay, p. 338.

[n] Inquiry, p. 292.

of the devil what his name was, and I allow this to be an objection againſt that falſe ſuppoſition; then you affirm, that I *treat the inſpired penmen no leſs diſreſpectfully than that unbeliever* [o]; though you knew, that the queſtion did not concern the *reſpect* due to the Evangeliſts, but their *meaning* only; and that I was attempting to aſſign ſuch a meaning to their language, as would effectually reſcue them from the ſcorn of unbelievers.

You are pleaſed to join me with *Celſus* (whom you juſtly call *one of the bittereſt enemies Chriſtianity ever had*); for you ſay, *you are truly grieved to find his calumny of* Mary Magdalen *catched up, and faſtened upon her by a miniſter of Chriſt* [p]. Profeſſions of being *truly grieved* for the perſon they mean to injure, are the uſual artifice of all ſlanderers, in order to gain credit to ſome improbable and groundleſs calumny. And though your grief may be more ſincere, it was not your averſion to calumny, that prevented you from diſcern-

[o] Inq. p. 37; ſee alſo p. 24, 25, 314.   [p] Inq. p. 85.

ing

ing the true ſtate of the caſe; which is as follows: Celſus, in order to diſparage the evidence of Chriſt's reſurrection, aſks, *Who ſaw him after he was riſen with the marks of his crucifixion?* and then returns the following anſwer: *Why, a diſtracted woman, as you ſay, or confeſs*[q]. This expreſſion implies, that Mary Magdalen was diſtracted at the time of Chriſt's appearing to her after his reſurrection; and therefore was, what Origen repreſents it, a calumny[r], that had no foundation in Scripure[s]; for ſhe was in her right mind at that time, having been cured long before. With what truth then could you affirm, that I[t] had faſtened upon

[q] τίς τȣτο οἶδε; *(al.* εἶδε;*)* γυνὴ πάροιϛρος, ὡς φατὶ. The laſt words are juſtly rendered by Spencer (who had not your end to anſwer, by perverting their obvious meaning), *ut ipſi fatemini*. Origen, c. Celſ. l. 2. p. 94. And in p. 96. *veſtrâ quoque confeſſione*. The expreſſion is not, as you would explain it, *(Inq. p.* 85, *note)* an *inſinuation*, but a direct aſſertion, *that the Chriſtians acknowledged, that the woman was diſturbed in her ſenſes.*

[r] Origen, c. Celſ. p. 96.   [s] Id. p. 97.   [t] Eſſay, p. 105.

her the calumny of Celsus? You were not ignorant, that I cited his account of her merely to shew, that the expression of having *seven demons*, to which Celsus here refers, was, in ancient times, understood to denote *a violent phrenzy*. Thus it certainly was understood by Celsus; and, according to him, by the primitive Christians. Origen does not intimate, that she had never been disturbed in her senses; nor can you, Sir, say she never had, whether her insanity proceeded from natural causes, or from demoniacal possession. Her former disorder, in either case, implied no reflection upon her moral character, which Celsus spared, but which you, without any reason, have impeached; accusing her of having been *a great and enormous sinner*.[u]

You farther represent the author of the Essay, and those who broach the same opinions, as *acting the part of confederates with the devil*[x]; as being *the emissaries whom he employs to argue, and banter us out of our*

[u] Inquiry, p. 83.   [x] Inq. p. 335.

belief

belief of possessions, and as persons who *may have the devil at their elbow* [y]; and you earnestly intreat them to consider whether this may not be the case. When the lower part of mankind reproach one another with having *the devil at their elbows, and with having the devil in them,* you think it right to reprove their profaneness. But when you see fit to adopt their language, we must consider it as the effusion of piety and benevolence. You assure the world, after expressing your concern lest I should be guilty of the irremissible sin, that *if any brother be guilty of the sin that is not unto death, he hath your most earnest prayers to God, that it may not be imputed to him* [z]. This is kind; almost beyond belief. It is indeed, a new phenomenon in the history of the human mind, for which our moral philosophers will find it difficult to account, that you should be able at the same instant both to bear the same person so much ill-

[y] Inq. p. 213. See also p. 209, 210.
[z] Inq. p. 71, 72.

will, as ſtudiouſly to load him with falſe accuſations, and ſo much good-will as to pray moſt earneſtly to God for his pardon. *Doth a fountain ſend forth at the ſame place ſweet water and bitter* *? In this cenſorious age, many perhaps may be too forward to ſuſpect, that in ſome caſes airs of piety are aſſumed to impoſe upon weak minds, and that prayer itſelf is nothing more than a commodious vehicle for ſlander. Inconſideration is the only apology that can be made, for ſuch a ſtrange mixture of malevolence and Chriſtian charity.

In your zeal to aſperſe the author of the *Eſſay*, you ſay, that *to a fair deſcription of our Saviour's miracles on the demoniacs, I have tacked a collection of the low, indecent, juggling tricks of profane exorciſts and magicians; without* ANY SALVO *to prevent their being paralleled with each other; and that this is done at the concluſion of my performance, that the idea of theſe ſilly, and ridiculous charms, might be left, in a manner, laſt upon the minds of the readers* [a]. You could not be ignorant, that in the very part

* James iii. 11.   [a] Inq. p. 219.

of the *Essay* to which you refer on this occasion [b], I set myself to point out the manifest difference, in several respects, between Christ's cure of demoniacs, and the juggling tricks of prophane exorcists [c], on purpose to prevent their being paralleled with each other, which they never can be on my principles, though they may on your's. I was totally at a loss to account for so very extraordinary a misrepresentation of my sentiments, till I discovered your design, which plainly appears from what immediately follows the foregoing citation from you: *This is such management, as must raise the indignation of every serious Christian* [d]. Your design was as honourable, as were the means you used to accomplish it. With what other view, than

[b] Essay, p. 408.

[c] The difference between the exorcists and our Saviour consisted, as was shewn in the Essay, in this; that the former only pretended to drive away demons by the use of certain charms; the latter cured those violent disorders anciently ascribed to the possession of demons, without the use of charms, or natural remedies, by a sovereign word alone. Essay, p. 408—416.

[d] Inquiry, p. 219.

that

that of awakening an unjuft refentment in every honeft man againft the author of the *Effay*, could you affirm, without any colour for the accufation, that *the principle which runs through it, can be none other than this, or to this effect: that it is allowable to profefs one thing, and believe the contrary* [e] ?

I leave it to you, to reconcile your treatment of your opponents with candour and integrity. Should I happen to forget the refpect due to your age, your profeffion, your rank, and general character in life; you will remember that you have fet the example. For by ftooping to the loweft arts of controverfy, you forgot the refpect that you owed to yourfelf.

I readily allow, that even to *you*, Sir, every favourable allowance fhould be made, that the nature of the cafe admits. Rather than, I fhould impeach your veracity [f], I would

[e] Inquiry, p. 124.

[f] I cannot (in any manner honourable to you) account for the following mifreprefentation of Mr. Jofeph Mede, however ambitious you might be of fupporting your argument by his great authority. You tell the world, (Inq. p. 185) that Mr. Mede fays,

I would ascribe your defamatory and injurious language to the influence of prejudice and paſſion, (from which ſcarce are any totally

The word δαιμονιον is in the Scripture never taken in the better, or indifferent ſenſe, however profane authors do uſe it; but always in an evil ſenſe, for the devil, or an evil ſpirit. Theſe are, indeed, the very words of Mr. Mede; and you refer us to the place in his works where they may be found, (which in the fourth edition is p. 634.) This has the appearance of fair dealing. Nevertheleſs, incredible as it muſt appear to ſome, Mr. Mede's opinion was the very reverſe of that which you aſcribe to him; for the point he undertook to prove was, as he himſelf expreſſes it, *that the word δαιμονιον is ſometimes in Scripture taken according to the theology of the Gentiles, and not always for an evil ſpirit.* In the paſſage that you cite from him as expreſſive of his own opinion, he profeſſes to be only ſtating an objection againſt it; for he introduces it with ſaying, *ſome things in our way muſt firſt be cleared.* And after ſtating the objection, he immediately proceeds to anſwer it; and ſhews from Acts xvii. 18. Rev. ix. 13. 1 Cor. x. 21, as he had before done from 1 Tim. iv. 1, that demon is not always uſed for an evil ſpirit. As juſtly, Sir, might I appeal to *your authority* in ſupport of my opinion on the ſubject about which we differ, becauſe you ſometimes ſtate my objections againſt it; as you, on the ſame ground, appeal to Mr. *Mede's authority* in ſupport of your opinion, which he diſavows and refutes.

As

totally exempt, but) which so diſtort the human underſtanding, as to make things appear quite different from what they really are. But, indeed, Sir, you have taken very little care, to exemplify in your

As little, Sir, am I able to account for the following miſrepreſentation of myſelf, (Inquiry, p. 180, 181, 182.) where you charge me with *artfully inſinuating*, that the ſacred writers themſelves regarded thoſe as deified ſpirits, whom the Heathens conſidered as ſuch, merely becauſe I had ſaid, what you allow to be true, that the ſacred writers employ the term demon to deſcribe the heathen gods, or ſuch human ſpirits as the Gentiles deified. Such an *inſinuation* as you reproach me with, had it been contained in my words, could not have proceeded from *art*, but muſt have been the ſole effect of the moſt extreme *folly*; becauſe it would have been a contradiction to every page of my writings. But, in fact, there is not the leaſt colour for your accuſation; for beſides my making the moſt explicit declarations (Eſſay, p. 326, and in other places) that the prophets of God gave the objects of heathen worſhip the ſame titles as the Heathens did, merely to characteriſe, not to allow, the pretenſions of thoſe objects of their worſhip; beſides this, thoſe very pretenſions were expreſsly rejected by me, upon the authority of the ſacred writers; as you could not but know, when you undertook to anſwer what I had urged to ſhew, that *demons were nothing in the world*. Such miſrepreſentations as theſe ſtand in need of an uncommon meaſure of candour and indulgence.

own conduct, the principle you would eſtabliſh, " that controverſy is carried on in the preſent age with more decency and good manners, than in any former period of time." It is with a very ill grace, that you [g] reproach the firſt reformers with *virulence* and *acrimony* in their controverſial writings. Men's paſſions were at that time generally agitated in an uncommon degree, which is ſome apology for the reformers.

You tell your opponents, that *the queſtion ought to be debated with great caution and candour* [h]. Surely candour is due not only *to* you, but alſo *from* you to thoſe who have the ſame reverence for the ſacred oracles with yourſelf, and only wiſh to clear them from the objections of our common adverſaries. You plead your good intention [i] in your own favour, when you thought yourſelf treated with undeſerved ſeverity by your opponents. Your cauſe would not have ſuffered any injury, had

[g] Worthington on Redemption, p. 136.
[h] Inquiry p. 222.
[i] Dr. Worthington on Redemption, p. 412. note.

you defended it with the calmnefs of a philofopher, and the candour of a Chriftian.

I could wifh you to review the controverfy. For while your mind was agitated by ftrong (but groundlefs [k]) refentments, how was it poffible for you to hold the balance of your judgment with an even and fteady hand? With refpect to your readers, do you not difcern the impropriety of attempting to inflame their paffions and prejudices, in order to create in them an equal incapacity of judging truly concerning the point in queftion? This, at beft, was a needlefs undertaking: for the prejudices of education, which were all on your fide of the queftion [l], do, of their own accord, obftruct conviction; and are generally too ftubborn, to yield to the moft forcible reafoning, and the moft engaging addrefs. I am, Rev. SIR,

Your moft humble fervant,

H. FARMER.

[k] I may borrow your complaint againft Dr. Grey, *The whole ground of your quarrel with me, is, that I have prefumed to differ from you.* Id. ib.

[l] Inquiry, p. 117, 216.

LETTER II.

Reverend Sir,

YOUR *abuse* of the advocates for the antidemoniac system, reflecting dishonour on none but yourself, I shall drop the subject, and proceed to consider your *reasonings* against the system itself. It will be proper to begin with examining your objections against the account I had given of POSSESSING DEMONS.

What the author of the *Essay* undertook to prove, was this: "That the possessing demons spoken of in the New Testament, were the deities of the Heathens, or such human spirits as, after the dissolution of their bodies, were supposed to be converted into demons." On the other hand, you, in your *Inquiry*, refer possessions to the devil; you assert, that "he is the chief author of them[a]; and attempt to justify the English translation,

---
[a] Inquiry, p. 189, 190.

translation, in rendering the Greek word *demon* by *devils*[b]. By the devil you understand the *chief* of the fallen angels[c]. You affirm, " That as God is the author of all good, so the devil is the author of all evil[d]; and that " he is justly to be reckoned the evil principle[e]."

In support of his opinion, the author of the *Essay*[f] observes, that the Scripture never describes more than one evil spirit by the word devil; and never represents any persons as possessed by the *devil*, or by *devils*, not even in a single instance, notwithstanding the great frequency with which the evangelists speak on the subject of possessions. In all the instances in which the term *devils* occurs in the English translation of the New Testament, the original word is *demons*[g], and not that from whence comes the English word *devil*[h]. In order to determine who these

---

[b] Inquiry, p. 152, 187. [c] Inq. p. 63, 227, 228.
[d] Inq. p. 233. [e] Inq. p. 233, 306. [f] Essay, ch. 1. sect. 1.
[g] δαιμονες, δαιμονια, δαιμονιζομενοι. [h] διαβολος.

demons

demons were, it was shewn in the *Essay*[i], that the ancient Heathens and Jews, and the primitive Christians, did all agree in representing them as no other than human spirits. From these premises, the following conclusion was drawn; viz. " That the sacred writers, having given us no notice of their using the word in a new or peculiar sense, did certainly employ it in reference to possessions, in the same sense in which all other persons did." To suppose the contrary, would be to suppose, that they intended to deceive their readers. It is the more necessary to allow, that the Evangelists, when speaking of possessing demons, did not refer to any other than human spirits, as they knew that to such spirits the term demons was applied by the Heathens,[k] and by the authors of the Septuagint.[l] Nay, they have themselves used it to describe such dead men as the super-

---

[i] Essay, ch. 1. sect. 2.
[k] Acts, xvii. 18, 22.   Dissert. on Miracles, p. 203, note (q).   [l] Deut. xxxii. 17. Psalm. cvi. 37. Essay, p. 223, note (m).

stition

stition of the Heathens deified[m], and corrupt Christians have proposed as objects of worship[n]. It can bear no other meaning in any of the passages in the New Testament, in which it occurs without having any relation to possessions; as was shewn by a distinct examination of each[o].

I now proceed to consider your several *objections* against the foregoing account of possessing demons. You have thrown them together in some confusion; but they may all be comprehended under the following divisions; such as are drawn from the heathen philosophers, from the ancient Jews, from Christ and his apostles, and from the primitive Christians.

I. You undertake to shew, that (δαιμων) *demon is a name belonging to the devil, and given to him by ancient* HEATHEN *writers of good authority*[p].

All[q] that you have offered under this head, you seem to have taken too much

[m] 1 Cor. x. 20, 21.
[n] 1 Tim. iv. 1. Rev. ix. 20. Essay, p. 209, 218.
[o] Ib. 208—219.
[p] Inq. p. 153, and App. 328.
[q] Inquiry, p. 153—155, 159, 168.

upon truft: for you do not always cite the words of your authors; very feldom refer to the places in which their words may be found; and content yourfelf with the account given of them by others, in cafes in which you ought to have had immediate recourfe to the authors themfelves. You even appeal to fpurious books, in proof of the fentiments of the authors to whom they are falfely afcribed. Such, probably, is the *Philofophy of Oracles*, afcribed to Porphyry[r]; and fuch certainly are all the works that pafs under the name of Hermes Trifmegiftus. The learned Bifhop of of Gloucefter, and others, fuppofe the latter to be in part the forgery of fome heretical Chriftian[s]. Neverthelefs, inftead of giving your readers notice of this, you set out with declaring, that you made your appeal to writers of *good authority*[t]; and even diftinguifh Hermes from the reft, as a *very ancient authority*[u]. You have my leave, however, to avail yourfelf of all

---

[r] See Lardner's Jewifh and Heathen Teftim. vol. iii. ch. xxxvii [s] Div. Legat. vol. I. part 2, p. 233, 5th edit. [t] Inq. p. 153. [u] Inq. p. 154.

your authorities; but you will scarce thank me for this permission, if you see fit to weigh the following particulars:

1. *Demon* is never used by the Heathens as the proper name of any one particular being. It is a word of general import, denoting a *deity*[w]; and employed indifferently, in a good and in a bad sense[x]; as is acknowledg-ledged by Plutarch[y], in that very treatise to which you refer, as containing a proof, that *demon* is a name to which the devil is emi-nently[z] intitled. So far is it from being true, as you affirm, that he may be called demon *paramount*[a]; that the supreme deity of the Heathens, Jupiter, styled *The Ruler of the world*, is called the *greatest demon*[b].

[w] Dissert. on Miracles, p. 174.
[x] Ibid. p. 204. Plato (Convivium, p. 327. ed. Ficini. Lugd. 1590) says there were different sorts of demons, ὕτοι δὴ οἱ δαίμονες πολλοὶ καὶ παντοδαποί εἰσιν.
[y] De Is. & Osir. p. 360, 361. τῷ δὲ ἀπὸ τῶν δαιμόνων προσρήματι χρωμένη κοινῶς ἐπί τε χρηστῶν καὶ φαύλων.
[z] κατ' ἐξοχὴν, Inquiry, p. 153.
[a] Inquiry, p. 154.
[b] Πάντες οὖν οἱ κατὰ τοὺς τόπους συνάρχοντες τῷ μεγίστῳ δαίμονι θεοί. Omnes igitur secundum loca unà cum dæmone maximo imperium tenent dii, Plato in Politico. *Jupiter, the father of gods and men*, is called a demon by Hesiod (de Scuto

The word demon is often ufed as equivalent to *god*,* by Homer, and other writers; though the Heathens fometimes diftinguifhed between gods and demons[a]. When it is ufed in a bad fenfe, fome epithet is joined with it; but it is not then appropriated to any one evil demon in particular. So far is it from being true, that demon was a name peculiarly belonging to the devil, amongft the Heathens, that had they had any knowledge of him, they could no more diftinguifh him by this name from other demons, than they could diftinguifh Peter or John from the reft of the human fpecies, by calling him a man.

2. When the word demon is applied to *wicked* fpirits, we are not from hence to

---

Scuto Herculis, v. 89, 94, 103.) and Theognis, (Sentent. v. 149) and others.

* θεος.

[a] Plutarch, p. 361, fpeaks of fome who were changed from demons into gods, and of others who were worfhipped with the honours due to both. See *Differt. on Miracle*, p. 183.

[b] Such as   , and ταυλος. See *Differt. on Miracles*, p. 205. in the note. Good demons are alfo diftinguifhed by fuitable epithets.

conclude,

conclude, that thefe fpirits were originally of a higher order than mankind. For it was a very prevailing opinion amongſt the ancient philofophers, that as the departed fouls of good men became good demons, fo thofe of wicked men became wicked demons [d]. Neverthelefs, whenever you meet with a wicked demon[e], in the writings of the Heathens, you inftantly conclude that the devil was intended, though you are forced to own, that they could have no knowledge of him [f]. You even fuppofe, that thofe who delivered oracles were infpired by a devil [g]; evident as it is, that the heathen gods, to whom

[d] Diſſert. on Miracles, p. 208. Compare the citation from Philo. p. 207, note (*.)

[e] You cannot infer *merely* from the mention even of *evil angels* in the writings of the ancients, that apoftate angels are intended. The Heathens called the fame fpirits indifferently angels, or demons, or heroes. *Diſſert. on Miracles*, p. 181.

[f] See Inquiry, p. 162. Plato, you fay, confeſſed that the knowledge of them (demons), and of their origin, was above his comprehenfion.

[g] Ap. to Inq. p. 317.

oracles

oracles were most commonly ascribed, were deified men [h].

3. The most that all your authorities will prove, is, that several of the heathen philosophers asserted the existence of evil demons, of a nature superior to the human species [i], and their subjection to a prince and ruler. This fact may be supported, though not by the spurious testimony of

[h] Essay, p. 22.

[i] I admitted (Essay, p. 49. note), that *several* philosophers taught that the *heathen demons*, or deities, were not really deities, or gods, but evil spirits, of a rank superior to mankind. But you misrepresent me, when you say, *Inq. p.* 172, " that I acknowledge the *wisest* and *best* of the ancient philosophers taught, that the demons in *general* were evil spirits of a rank superior to mankind." In another place, you still more grosly misrepresent me, as maintaining, " that demons were *always* taken to signify departed souls," *Inq. p.* 161. I never said this of any but *possessing* demons. And though I admitted, that *several* philosophers asserted the existence of superior demons, I never imagined that these philosophers were *wiser* than the rest, or that they believed there were no other demons than those of the highest order. Instead, therefore, of admitting your charge of having contradicted myself, I might complain, with no small reason, of your misrepresentation.

Hermes

Hermes and Porphyry, yet by that of other writers [k]. But though we admit the fact, we can not allow the consequence you would draw from it, *that all evil demons were esteemed to be none other than fallen angels, long before the Gospel appeared in the world* [l]. For we have seen that the Heathens taught, that many human souls became wicked demons. As to their superior demons, you have not shewn that they are the same with the fallen angels referred to in Scripture. This is a point you can never prove; and which I would caution you against attempting to prove, lest you should hurt your own cause. For these demons were considered by the Heathens as the authors of evil to mankind; and were worshipped by them as gods [m]. Now, the Scripture asserts the utter

[k] See Dissert. on Miracles, p. 183, 204, in note (¹), and p. 220, note (ʳ).

[l] Inq. p. 154, 155.

[m] The Heathens divided (τὸ θεῖον) the godhead into divinities *beneficial* and *hurtful*, εἰς τὸ βλάπτον καὶ τὸ ὠφελοῦν. The caco-demons of the Greeks, and the vejoves & numina læva of the Romans, like the Arimanius of the Persians, and the evil principle of other eastern nations, were worshipped under the character of malignant beings.

impotence of all their gods; and in direct opposition to the notion of their being the authors of evil, declares that Jehovah *forms the light, and creates darkness:* that *he makes peace, and creates evil*[n]. Some suppose, that, in this passage, there is a peculiar reference to the evil principle held by the Persians. Now, if this evil principle was the devil, it will follow from hence, that, according to Isaiah, the devil can not be, what you represent him, the author of natural evil. Indeed, the prophet refers all natural evil, as well as natural good, to God. Most certainly the demons, whom the Heathens represented as the authors of all evil, do not answer to the idea of those fallen angels who are confined in chains of darkness to the judgment of the great day. And even were it true, that the higher rank of demons amongst the Heathens were fallen angels; this would not serve your purpose:

4. For after all your learned researches, you have not been able to produce a single instance of any heathen writer's referring possessions to evil demons superior to

[n] If. xlv. 7.

man-

mankind; though one such instance would have served your cause, more than all you have offered in it's support. You say*, indeed, that " according to the doctrine of the Essay, the twelve greater gods ᵖ, vulgarly supposed to have been deified mortals, were possessing demons. But these in Plato's estimation existed from all eternity." Your argument proceeds on two suppositions highly extravagant. It supposes, that because possessing demons were considered by the Heathens as deified men; therefore all deified men were possessing demons: and it farther supposes, that we are to form our judgment of the twelve greater gods, by the speculations ᑫ of a philosopher who rejected the common opinion concerning them, merely because he deemed it absurd; rather than by the whole current of heathen antiquity, and the declarations of Scripture, which represent all the heathen gods as dead men. You likewise appeal to Apuleius and Por-

* Inq. p. 162.
ᵖ Dii majorum gentium.
ᑫ See Dissert. on Mir. p. 189.

phyry

phyry [r], as describing possessing demons as middle powers between the gods and men. The latter, according to your own account of him, speaks chiefly of demons entering the bodies of men, in order to regale themselves with human ordure, which, your author tells you, is their chief delight. But this has no relation to possessions [s]; nor can I conceive why you mentioned it, unless it was to expose Porphyry to the contempt of your readers. As to Apuleius, you could scarce have quoted a stronger authority against yourself. The heathen philosophers held that there were different kinds of demons [t]; that some of them were spiritual substances of a more noble origin than the human race [u], and that

---

[r] Inq. p. 163.

[s] You say, (Inq. p. 163.) that according to Porphyry, "their *houses* were full of demons, and their *bodies* likewise." This passage, even were it genuine, would only prove, (what will be shewn in the 3d letter) that the Heathens did not esteem every thing possessed that had demons in it; for those houses which were full of demons, were never said to be possessed.

[t] Varias species dæmonum a philosophis perhiberi, Apuleius De Deo Socratis, p. 686, 687, ed. Delphin. See above, p. 29, note (x).

[u] Id. p. 684, 690.

others had once been men[x]. Of both thefe kinds of demons, fome (as we have feen) were good, others evil; and thofe of each kind were united under a prince and leader, or had their refpective demonarch[y]. It muſt be obſerved farther, that different orders of demons had different

[x] Eſt et fecundo fignificatu ſpecies dæmonum, animus humanus, &c. Id. p. 688.

[y] That ſuch demons as were of human origin had a prince, according to the Heathens, appears from the Alceſtis of Euripides, where Hercules is introduced as ſaying, μάχην συνάψας δαιμόνων τῶ κοιράνω, which the ſcholiaſt explains by τῶ τῶν νεκρῶν κυρίω. This prince was called by the Heathens, Pluto. Could any credit be given to the forgery that paſſes under the name of Porphyry, (apud Euſeb. Præp. Ev. l. 4. c. 23.) the prince of the higher race of demons was called Sarapis. But according to Plutarch, (de If. & Oſir. p. 361, D.) Sarapis was no other than Pluto. Sammael was worſhipped by the ancient Zabians as the Prince of evil demons, Hottinger. Hiſt. Oriental. l. 1. c. 8. The Perſians had their Arimanius. Plato thought that the cauſe of evil was the moving principle that reſided in matter. (See Bayle under the article Zoroaſter). This very principle is called by Manes (in his epiſtle on the foundation, ap. Aug. contr. ep. Manich. c. 15. n. 19.) immanis princeps et dux, habens circa ſe innumerabiles principes, quorum omnium ipſe erat mens atque origo. To which of theſe demonarchs does your idea of the devil anſwer? The independent principle

ferent stations and employments respectively assigned them [z]; so that those of one order did not usurp the office of another. To which order then belonged the office of possession? You shall learn that from your own voucher, Apuleius[*]: he tells us,

of evil is called by Plutarch (De Placit. Philos. l. 1, c. 7. p. 881. E.) *an evil demon.* But you justly censure the doctrine of *two independent principles,* as both *absurd and impious.* Worthington on Redemption, p.410.

[z] See Apuleius, de Deo Socratis, p. 677, &c. & p. 689, 690. Compare Plato's account of the different functions of demons, Oper. p. 327, ed. Ficini. Lugd. What is said above concerning different orders of demons, is true concerning demons of the same order, or such as were of human origin; they had different offices assigned them, as appears from the following note.

[*] Ex lemuribus, qui posterorum suorum curam sortitus, placato & quieto numine domum possidet, Lar dicitur familiaris. Qui verò ob adversa vitæ merita, nullis bonis sedibus, incerta vagatione ceu quodam exilio punitur, inane terriculamentum bonis hominibus, cæterum noxium malis: id genus plerique larvas perhibent, p. 688, 689. He soon after adds, Quippè tantùm eos deos appellant, qui ex eodem numero justè & prudenter vitæ curriculo gubernato, pro numine posteà ab hominibus proditi, fanis & cæremonijs vulgo advertuntur: ut in Bæotiâ Amphiaraus, in Africâ Mopsus. A plain proof that oracles were ascribed to human spirits.

that

that the ghosts of the deceased were distinguished by different names, according to their different functions. The harmless ghosts were called *lares*; and the mischievous ones, *larvæ*. Now, it is allowed on all hands, that the larvati were so called from larva; and they exactly answer to the demoniacs of the New Testament.

I have now examined all your heathen authorities; and have shewn, that they are either spurious, or foreign from your purpose, or that they conclude against you. How little reason then had you to represent me, as " seeming to adopt the opinion of the Heathens in general, in opposition to that of the philosophers; and, as having only the ignorant vulgar to keep me in countenance[a]?" Had this been the case, I might have pleaded, that the language of the New Testament is not borrowed from the schools of philosophy, but from common life. But for any thing that has hitherto appeared to the contrary, the learned and illiterate were all of one

[a] Inquiry, p. 161.

opinion on the subject before us, and the demons in question were *universally* considered, throughout the ancient heathen world, as the souls of deified men. In a word, the evidence, and that as clear and cogent as can be desired, is all on one side of the question.

I agree with you, that the writers of the New Testament were not to be taught by unenlightened Heathens[b]. Nevertheless, they learned the meaning of words in vulgar use, as all other persons did, and employed them in the same sense. And in order to know whether the Greek word demon, when employed in reference to possession, did universally bear one uniform meaning in the time of Christ, it was necessary to shew, how it was understood by the Heathens as well as by the Jews; especially, as the evangelists wrote in the Greek language, which, at the commencement of the Christian æra, was in general use amongst the Heathens. You, Sir, no less than myself, have appealed to the

[b] Inq. p. 173, 181.

Heathens

Heathens to determine the meaning of the New Teſtament language; and, you go farther than I have done: for, whenever they appear to you to favour your opinion, you ſeem willing to allow, that they derived their information, though not from reaſon, yet, in ſome meaſure, from tradition c.

II. I will now proceed to vindicate and confirm the account given in the *Eſſay* of the ſentiments entertained of poſſeſſing demons by the JEWS.

Againſt the teſtimony of Joſephus d, who in the moſt expreſs terms tells us, that the demons in queſtion were *departed ſouls*, you have not raiſed any objection. But you ſeem not to approve the account which the *Eſſay* e gives of Beelzebub; and pleaſantly tell f your readers, that they are to infer from it, " that ſuch a *poor* devil can have but little influence upon men." It muſt on all hands be allowed, that Beelzebub was conſidered by the Phariſees as

c Inq. p. 327. d Cited in the Eſſay, p. 42.
e Eſſay, p. 14--17, and p. 30--40. f Inq. p. 60, 61.

the

the prince of possessing demons. But, according to Josephus, who was himself a Pharisee, possessing demons were human spirits. Such, therefore, was their prince and leader. It has been observed[h], that Beelzebub was the name given to the god of Ekron, or Accaron, who had a temple and oracle there; and, therefore, must have been a man. For such all the heathen deities had really been; those, especially, to whom divination and oracles were ascribed[i]. Nay, you admit[k] (what I had shewn to be very probable[l]), that Beelzebub is the same as Pluto, who is well known to be the son of Saturn, and brother of Jupiter and Neptune, and was called the chief and ruler of the infernal gods, or departed spirits[m].

In

[h] Essay, p. 31.   [i] Essay, p. 39.   [k] Inq. p. 49.
[l] Essay, p. 40, note *y*).
[m] Pluto was called Summanus, q. summus manium, August. de Civ. Dei, l. iv. c. 23. See Essay, p. 40. The learned Jurieu (Hist. critic. dogm. & cult. &c. part iv. c. iii. p. 632, seq.) as cited by Buddeus (Hist. Ecclef. tom. ii. p. 526), was of opinion that Beelzebub was Pluto, the prince deorum manium, seu deorum

In confirmation of what was advanced in the Essay with respect to the Jews, two farther observations may be made. First of all, it is highly probable in itself, that the Jews entertained the same sentiments with respect to possessing demons as the Heathens; for, the former not only adopted the principles of the latter on other subjects, but they did this in reference to demons. Even you[m] admit, that they borrowed, in one instance, from the heathen demonology. And whoever is acquainted with the *Greek* versions of the Old Testament, and the Alexandrian in particular, usually called the Septuagint, must have observed, in a great number of in-

---

deorum infernalium. Pluto, he observes, is sometimes called Acheron (which he derives from Accaron), particularly in that line of Virgil:

Flectere si nequeo superos, Acheronta movebo.

Pluto was certainly worshipped in Phœnicia, (as appears from the testimony of Sanchoniatho, apud Euseb. Præp. Ev. l. i. c. 10.); and the oracle that Ahaziah sent to consult (2 Kings i. 1.) was in his temple, where the dead were evoked; which species of divination was called νεκρομαντεια, and ψυχομαντεια. Buddeus, ubi supra.

[m] Inquiry, p. 48.

stances,

stances, a striking conformity between the demons there described, and those of the Heathens[n]. The same observations may be applied, and in a greater degree, to the *Chaldee*[o] translations and paraphrases of the Old

---

[n] The Septuagint, from a fondness for demonism, renders several very different Hebrew words by *demon*, though not one of them be capable of that meaning; particularly *seirim*. Is. xiii. 21. *schedim*, Deut. xxxii. 17. Ps. cv. 35. *elilim*, Ps. xcv. 5. *ziim*, Is. xxxiv. 14. It introduces the *fabulous* monsters of the Gentile theology, (Is. xxxiv. 13. συναντήσουσι δαιμόνια ὀνοκευταύροις); and countenances the ridiculous distinction between morning, mid-day, and nocturnal demons, Ps. xci. 6. Many other examples might be mentioned.

[o] The general doctrine of evil spirits is obtruded upon the Scriptures, by the targum of Jonathan B. Uziel, on Leviticus, xvii. 7. and Deut. xxxii. 10, 17; by the targum of Onkelos on Deut. xxxii. 14; and the Chaldee paraphrase, Is. xxxiv. 14. The text is made to assert the several different sorts of spirits, which the fables of the Heathens described, hags, fairies, hobgoblins, spectres, demons famished with hunger, and howling in the wilderness; targum of Jonathan B. Uzziel on Deut. xxxii. 10, 24. Numb. vi. 24. After the Heathens, demons are distinguished into morning, mid-day, and nocturnal spirits; targum of Jonathan B. Uziel on Deut. xxxii. 24. Numb. vi. 24. Chaldee

(45)

Old Testament, (except the Targum, or Version of Onkelos, on the five books of Moses, though this is not free from blame). Both the Greek and the Chaldee versions, in the passages in which they introduce the heathen doctrine of demons, must be allowed by all to pervert the original text; and, consequently, the authors of those versions must have borrowed their demonology from the Heathens. Now, if this was certainly the case in many other instances, how can we doubt its being so with respect to that before us, their notion of possessing demons? For, as you observe on another occasion[p], " This notion being

---

24. Chaldee paraphrase of Pf. xci. 5. Pf. cxxi. 6. Song of Solomon iii. 8. c. iv. 6. Whenever these paraphrasts differ from the Heathens, it is in honour of their own nation. The Heathens thought that corn might be removed from one field to another by witchcraft; but ghosts and noxious spirits brought Solomon odoriferous trees from India; Chaldee par. Ecclef. ii. 5. And the Israelites, it seems, first invented the much admired art of putting to flight hurtful spirits; Song of Solomon iv. 6.

[p] Worthington on Redemption, p. 411.

spread

spread so much around them, it is no wonder if the Jews likewise were tinctured with it; it were rather to be wondered if they should escape it, notwithstanding they were otherwise taught." Secondly, what is so probable in theory, appears to be true in fact; for, not only did the authors of the Septuagint describe the dead men whom the Heathen worshipped, by the term demons; but we are told [q], that the Jewish doctors taught, "that the souls of the damned are for some time changed into demons, in order to be employed in tormenting mankind." They carried their conformity to the opinions of the Gentiles, so far as to assign to each species of demons a different prince and ruler. Beelzebub was the prince of possessing demons [r], and Samael was demonarch of the superior order of demons (and therefore could not be the same spirit with the former). Samael was the name which the Jews gave the devil; and they borrowed it from their

[q] See Calmet's Dictionary, under the article demon; and Theophylact, as cited by Grotius on Mat. viii. 28.
[r] Essay, p. 37, note (t).

neighbours in the east. According to the Jews, if we may credit St. Jerome[s], each band of demons had its demonarch. How very inconclusive then must all those reasonings be, which are built on the false supposition, that the Jews held only one prince of demons; and that demonarch was a term never applied by them to any but the devil?

III. You undertake to prove, that possessing demons were not human spirits, but apostate angels, by arguments drawn from the language of CHRIST AND HIS APOSTLES.

You defy any man to produce a single text, in which demon, when used with regard to possessions, signifies the soul of a departed man[t]. But I have shewn, that when used in this relation, it bore no other signification in the age and country in which the Gospel was published. And we have just the same reason to believe, that Christ

---

[s] St. Jerome (in Habac. iii. 5.) mentions it as a tradition of the Jews, Quomodo in evangelio, princeps dæmonum dicitur esse Beelzebub: ita *Reseph* dæmonis esse nomen, qui principatum teneat inter alios.

[t] Inquiry, p. 178.

and

and his apoftles ufed this word, as that they did any other, in its ordinary acceptation. Were we to allow, that they employed words in a fenfe peculiar to themfelves, without explaining their meaning, we muft necessarily grant, that they fpake in an unknown tongue.

You affirm, that " there are inftances in the New Teftament of the devil's poffeffing men under different names from that of demon[u]." The different *names* you here mean, are thofe of *Beelzebub* and *Satan*.

With regard to Beelzebub; as our Saviour never makes any mention of him but when he is either reafoning with the Pharifees upon their own principles[x], or alluding to their accufations; he cannot refer to a different fpirit from what they did, and therefore not to any other than a departed foul. Much lefs can it be fuppofed, that his idea of Beelzebub was different from that given us of him in the Old Teftament, as a heathen deity, or deified human fpirit; and, confequently, deftitute of all power

[u] Inquiry, p. 152, 155.
[x] See Effay, p. 331, note (i).

over

over mankind: a confideration, one would imagine, that would abate your zeal to prove him to be the devil. Many chriftian[y] writers, though they fuppofe Beelzebub to be one of the fallen angels, yet diftinguifh him from the devil, their prince and leader. Nor indeed has the Scripture ever confounded them together. But you fay, " Beelzebub and Satan are convertible terms,—and are confidered as names of one and the fame perfon[z]." If this be true, then fatan is nothing more than a heathen deity; for fuch we have proved Beelzebub to be.

But the term *fatan*, you plead, " is applied to the devil, as his proper name; and is as much appropriated to him as any proper name can be to any perfon[a]." Our Saviour, you obferve, called the devil by this name[b]: and add[c], that in one evangelift it is faid, *the devil put into the heart of Judas to betray Jefus**; and, that in another, we read, *that Satan entered*

---

[y] See Milton's Par. Loft, b. i. v. 80.   [z] Inq. p. 61.
[a] Inq. p. 61, 62, and 92, 93.   [b] Luke iv. 8.
[c] Inq. p. 91.   * John xiii. 2.

into

into Judas[d]. Still more fully to prove, that satan is the devil's proper name, you take notice[e], that the Hebrew word *satan*[f], in the Old Testament, is by the Septuagint translated *devil*[g], no less than seventeen times. This seems plausible, but will not, perhaps, bear examination.

The Hebrew word *satan* denotes *an adversary*[h], and with the emphatic article prefixed to it, *the adversary*. It may be applied emphatically to any one particular enemy, to the devil, for example: but it is not appropriated to him; it is no more

---

[d] Luke xxii. 3.   [e] Inq. p. 155, 156.
[f] שטן   [g] διάβολος

[h] Ὁ δ' Ἑβραίων διαλέκτω σαταν, καὶ Ἑλληνικώτερον ὑπό τινων ὀνομασθεὶς σατανᾶς, μεταλαμβανόμενος εἰς Ἑλλάδα φωνὴν ἐστιν ἀντικείμενος. Πᾶς δ' ὁ τὴν κακίαν ἑλόμενος, καὶ τὸν κατ' αὐτὴν βίον, ὡς τὰ ἐναντία πράττων τῇ ἀρετῇ, σατανᾶς ἐστιν, τοῦτ' ἐστιν, ἀντικείμενος τῷ υἱῷ τοῦ θεοῦ, ὅτι δικαιοσύνη, καὶ ἀλήθεια καὶ σοφία. κυριώτερον δὲ ἀντικείμενος ἐστιν ὁ πρῶτος, κ. τ. λ. Ceterùm Satan, Hebræâ linguâ dictus, & à quibusdam formâ magis Græcanicà nominatus Satanas, interpretatur adversarius: omnis autem qui in vita sectatur malitiam, ut contrarius virtuti, Satanas est, hoc est, adversarius Dei filii, qui est *justitia, veritas, & sapientia:* sed magis propriè adversarius est is, qui primus omnium in pace beatè degentium amissis alis à beatitudine sua excidit. Origen. c. Celf. l. vi. p. 306.

his

his proper name, than it is that of any other perſon who acts the part of an adverſary. In the Old Teſtament, it is applied to a good angel, when acting an adverſe part[i]; and very frequently to men[k]. Examples of both theſe applications of the word were produced in the Eſſay, though you have taken no notice of them. The inſtances in which it has been ſuppoſed to refer to a malignant ſpirit, are but few[l]. Granting that it is ſometimes applied to ſuch

[i] Numb. xxii. 32, 33, cited in the Eſſay, p. 17, note (ˢ).

[k] Several inſtances of this application of the word ſatan, may be ſeen in that part of the Eſſay referred to above. I will add here, that it is uſed in the plural as well as in the ſingular number, Pſ. cix. 20. *Let this be the reward of* שטנ *mine adverſaries.* The ſame word occurs in v. 29, and in Pſ. xxxviii. 20. Pſ. lxxi. 13. Pſ. cix. 40. In theſe ſeveral places it is applied to men, and cannot poſſibly denote fallen angels.

[l] You ſay (Inq. p. 62.), "that the term ſatan is applied to the devil as his proper name, about ſix or ſeven times in the Old Teſtament;" but you have not referred us to the places where it is ſo applied. I do not recollect more than three occaſions on which it is commonly ſuppoſed to refer to an evil ſpirit; viz. in the hiſtory of Job ch. i. & ii. (where that word is frequently repeated)

such a *spirit*, yet it is no more his proper name, than it is the proper name of any of the *men* to whom it is applied. You might as well say, that the English words, an *enemy*, and an *opponent*, are the proper names of the prince of fallen angels, as to say the term *satan* is; for they are all used with equal latitude. Nor is it any just objection against this assertion, that the Septuagint translates satan by *devil*[m]; for the authors of that version use *devil* in the same latitude as the sacred writers do *satan*, as equivalent to adversary[n]; though your objection

---

repeated), in Zechariah iii. 1, 2. (where the margin of the English translation reads, *adversary*) and 1 Chron. xxi. 1. with the parallel places. And as you know, that some learned and eminent writers have contended, that even in these places there is no reference to the devil, it were to be wished, that instead of bare assertions, you had favoured the world with solid proofs of the truth of your interpretation of them.

[m] διαβολος.

[n] In Ps. cix. 6, we read, *set thou a wicked man over him, and let satan* (that is, an adversary, in the 70, διαβολος) *stand at his right hand:* which is thus explained by Bishop Patrick: "Let the worst man that can be found, be appointed to hear his cause when he

is

objection supposes, that they appropriate it to the prince of apostate angels.

In the New Testament, likewise, the term *satan* is given to such men as act the

is accused, and his most malicious adversary plead against him." There is here no reference to the chief of apostate spirits. Nor did the authors of the Septuagint imagine there was any reference to him in 1. Chron. xxi. 1. which they render καὶ ἀνέστη διάβολος (not ὁ διάβολος, ἐν τῷ ἰσραὴλ, *and there arose an enemy in Israel*. Even in reference to a good angel, the Hebrew word satan is translated διαβολὴ by the Septuagint, Numb. xxii. 32; which, therefore, must denote opposition without malice. In reference to the same angel, the Septuagint uses the verb from which διάβολος is derived, καὶ ἀνέστη ὁ ἄγγελος τοῦ Θεοῦ ἐνδιαβάλλειν αὐτὸν, Numb. xxii. 22. διαβαλεῖν, codex vatican.

Besides translating satan by διάβολος in cases in which men or good angels are spoken of, the Septuagint also renders other Hebrew words, particularly צר & צרר, by διάβολος, though they are never applied to that wicked spirit whom we call the devil. ὁ διάβολος is applied to Haman, the enemy of the Jews, in Esther vii. 4. ἐν γὰρ ἄξιος ὁ διάβολος τῆς αὐλῆς, and in c. viii. 1. ὅσα ὑπάρχει ἁμῶν τῷ διαβόλῳ. See also Aquila's version of Prov. xi. 13. and 1 Mac. i. 38. I will add, that the authors of the Septuagint, though they sometimes render Satan by διάβολος, yet, at other times, they preserve the Hebrew word itself, as in 3 Reg. xi. 14, 23, 25, in which places σατὰν is manifestly used concerning men. See also Syr. xxi. 29.

part of enemies, to calumniators and accusers. Though you are pleased to affirm [o] " that the term *satan* is applied to the devil about thirty-three times in the New Testament as his proper name;" yet you have not proved, that when it is applied to him there, it is ever used as his proper name. On the other hand, it often occurs as an appellative, and denotes in the New Testament, what it does in the Old, an *enemy* or *adversary* in general [p]. When the ancient Jews

---

[o] Inq. p. 62.

[p] I do not affirm, that the term *satan* does never refer to a wicked spirit; but I wish you had either cited or referred to the thirty-three places in the New Testament, in which you say it is applied to the devil. Were I to undertake to reduce their number, I should be supported by the authority of the Fathers. But, waving their authority, I am content to appeal to the natural and obvious import of a few passages. I shall begin with one on which you quote more than once. Inq. p. 62, 236. I refer to Rev. xii. 9. *The great dragon was cast out, that old serpent, called the devil, and satan, which deceiveth the whole world: he was cast out into the earth, and his angels were cast out with him.* This has been called the *history* of the devil's revolt; but it is certainly not a history, but a *prophecy*. St. John

Jews applied it to evil spirits, they did by no means confine it to any one in particular, nor John is not recording *past* events, but predicting *future* ones; and, should we grant, that it alludes to the common opinion concerning the expulsion of the devil from heaven, yet he cannot be the person here directly referred to. Great and oppressive powers are repre-presented in Scripture under the image of *serpents* and *dragons*, Pf. lxxiv. 13. If. xxvii. 1. Ezek. xxix. 1, 3. Luke x. 19. There is a peculiar propriety in repre-senting an *idolatrous* power under this figure, because serpents were the great objects of the antient idolatry, especially in the east. Of the idolatrous power, or dragon here spoken of, it is said, *that he is called devil* (διαβολος; without the article ὁ) *and satan*, that is, his power is *hostile* to Christians, and justifies its hostility against them by *false accusations*, which we know to have been the case in the early ages of christianity. This power *deceived the whole world*, had long sup-ported false religion in every country. *The war in heaven between Michael and his angels, and the dragon and his angels*, is allowed to denote the violent contention between the christian religion, and the powers that per-secuted it. The *defeat* of the latter is expressed by their being *cast out of heaven*: a manner of describing the loss of dignity and power familiar to the ancients, as is shewn in Essay, p. 334. Christians, in the time of Constantine, thought this prophecy accomplished by his advancement to the imperial throne, and the ex-clusion

nor even to any one species of them[1]. The word, therefore, is as applicable to the clusion of the heathen princes from it. The emperor Constantine himself says, that *the dragon was now removed*, Euseb. vit. Constant. l. ii. c. 46. It certainly denotes the downfal of some idolatrous and persecuting power, and the advancement of true religion. And because some enemy was still to arise, and bring new miseries upon the (Christian) world, it is said, *the devil*, the adversary, *is come down unto you in great wrath*, Rev. xii. 12. Those who apply these passages in the literal sense to the original expulsion of the devil from heaven, not only forget that they are *prophecies*, as was observed above, but also, that these prophecies are couched under allegorical representations. In other words, they do not consider, that the book of Revelations, by the consent of all interpreters, does not contain facts, but *visions*, or scenes presented to the apostle's imagination; and that these scenes were figurative and symbolical. In your sermons at Boyle's lectures, v. ii. p. 270, &c. you yourself do not reject a figurative interpretation of the passage we have been considering. By heaven you understand *great dignity*, particularly *the seat of the Roman empire*, p. 271. The seven heads of the dragon, you explain of the seven kings of Rome; and his seven horns you consider as *symbols of persecuting power*, p. 274, 275. Serpents and dragons, you say, were displayed on the military standards of the Romans, p. 276. The war in heaven, you explain of the contest between heathenism and christianity, the prince of possessing demons, as to the chief of fallen angels; and it is the *subject* alone

christinity, p. 286, 287. And you approve of those who make Licinius the great dragon in an inferior sense, or as the secondary agent in this war, p. 288. The devil's coming down in great wrath, you apply to Julian's furious attack upon Christianity, p. 290, 291.

There are other passages, in which an evil spirit cannot (I apprehend) be directly intended by *satan*. The term is applied to Peter as an appellative, by our Saviour: *Get thee behind me, Satan:* Mat. xvi. 23. St. Paul tells the Christians at Rome, *The God of peace shall bruise Satan* (the adversary) *under your feet shortly:* which Whitby, with great judgment, explains of the persecuting Jews, whose power was to be taken away by the destruction of Jerusalem. In 1 Thess. ii. 18. we read, *We would have come unto you once and again,* but *Satan* (the adversary) *hindered us.* The apostle here refers to the difficulties which the enemies of the gospel had laid in his way. The church at Pergamos is said to dwell where *Satan's seat* (or *throne* ὁ θρόνος) *is*; that is, where their enemies had great power; Rev. ii. 13. I need not multiply instances, and shall only, therefore, observe in general, that the English reader is misled by the translation now in use, which has preserved the original word *Satan*, which they ought to have rendered *adversary* in the New Testament, as they have often done in the Old: and indeed ought always to have done, even though the circumstances of the place

alone that muſt determine who the ſatan or adverſary is that is intended in any particular paſſage of Scripture, when it refers to evil ſpirits. If *poſſeſſion* be the ſubject, the ſatan, or enemy, is Beelzebub; if *temptation*, the ſatan, or enemy, is the devil. So little reaſon, Sir, had you to affirm*, that " the devil, ſatan and Beelzebub, are but different names for the prince of apoſtate angels!"

Nay, the term *devil* is not uſed in the New Teſtament as the proper name of any evil ſpirit. Aſmodeus and Samael were proper names, by the one or other of which the Jews diſtinguiſhed the chief of

---

place ſhould neceſſarily determine it to an evil ſpirit; for that particular application does not alter its general import. Perhaps the authors of this tranſlation did not ſufficiently advert to the frequent uſe of the ſingular number amongſt the Jews, in caſes in which we uſe the plural; and, conſequently, did themſelves imagine one particular being was meant by Satan, or the adverſary, where the manifeſt reference was to adverſaries in general. When St. Paul ſays, " Where is the wiſe? where is the ſcribe?" he means, where are the philoſophers of the Heathens? where are all the Jewiſh rabbies? See Eſſay, p. 335, and Joſh. ix. 1.

ᑫ They ſpeak of the prince of all the ſatans. Eſſay, p. 16, note (ʳ).   * Inq. p. 93.

the

the higher order of demons. But the term *devil**, like *satan*, is of general import; it denotes an *enemy*, a *prosecutor*, an *accuser*, and *calumniator*; and (though not always) is often applied to men. That it bears this application in the Greek version of the Old Testament[r], has been already shewn. I will here produce several passages from the New Testament, where it must be understood in the same manner. *Have I not chosen you twelve, and one of you is a devil*[s]? Christ here refers to the traitor, who was not the chief of fallen angels, but one who acted the part of an *enemy* in betraying his master. *Neither give place to the devil*[t], that is, give no occasion to the *railer*, or *slanderer* to reproach your religion: which is the sense given to this passage by Erasmus, and others. A bishop must not be a *novice*, or new convert, *lest being lifted up with pride, he fall into the condemnation of the devil*, or *calumniator*. Moreover, he *must have a good report of them which are without, lest he should fall into reproach, and*

---

* διαβολος.
[r] P. 52, note (n)   [s] John vi. 70.   [t] Ephes. iv. 27.

the snare of the devil[u], or the adversary and slanderer. It is hard to say, what peculiar advantage the devil might derive from a bishop's want of a good report of them that are without; but, it is easy to see, that this would expose him to the censure, and to the stratagems of the enemies of religion, who might try to shame him out of those principles, which served only to reproach and condemn him. Once more, *the devil* (the *enemies*, or *false accusers* of christianity) *shall cast some of you into prison*[x]. The term devil seems more especially to denote an *enemy of God*[y]. And in this sense it is applicable not only to wicked spirits, but to wicked men also; to such especially as corrupt or persecute true religion.

The term devil is used in the *plural number* in the New Testament, just as satan is in the Old, when it cannot refer to fallen

---

[u] 1 Tim. iii. 6, 7.   [x] Rev. ii. 10.

[y] Grotius (in 2 epist. ad Thessal. ii. 4.) explains ἀντικείμενος (which answers to διαβολος) by *Dei adversarius*; and adds, quomodo eximè vocatur diabolus et qui eum imitantur.

angels.

angels. St. Paul, in two of his epistles[z], forbids *women* to be *devils**. Will you affirm that the apostle designed to intimate that women are *angels*; and to guard them against becoming fallen angels? Must you not rather allow, that our translators were in the right, when they understood by devils, *slanderers and false accusers*, especially as the same word is applied to *men*[a]? *In the last time men will be devils*†. Without your assistance, Sir, I can never shew when this prophecy has been, or will be accomplished concerning *men*, according to your sense of devils; though too many answer the import of the word, as it denotes slanderers or false accusers. It is needless to produce more passages to prove, that the term devil is not (what you assert it to be) the proper name of one particular evil spirit. And if more evidence were wanted, you yourself have supplied it: for you have taken pains to shew, that

---

[z] 1 Tim. iii. 11. Tit. ii. 3.
* διαβόλους.
[a] 2 Tim. iii. 3.
† διάβολοι.

there

there were fix thoufand fix hundred and fixty-fix devils in one man[b]. So little reafon had you to reprefent the term devil as fo particularly defcriptive of the prince of fallen angels, *as not to admit of any miſtake, unleſs it be a wilful one*[c]. Here your judgment and temper keep pace together.

As to the particular *inſtances* you produce from the New Teſtament, of the devil's poſſeſſing men under different names from that of demon, they will fall more properly under confideration, when I come to explain the nature of poſſeſſions. Then I hope to fhew, that all your inſtances are foreign from the purpofe. Should this point be made good, the notion of poſſeſſing demons maintained in the Eſſay, will ſtand clear from all your objections againſt it, drawn from the New Teſtament.

What has been already offered on this fubject is fufficient to illuſtrate your great *modeſty* and *candour* in affirming[d], that NO

[b] Inq. p. 44.   [c] Inq. p. 62.   [d] Inq. p. 180.

HONEST

HONEST *man ever failed to find, or even doubted of it,* that is, of the sense in which the sacred writers use the word *demon,* by which you understand *the devil.* It is hard, indeed, if amongst all the eminent men who differ from you in this matter, there is not one as honest as the gentleman that passes this censure upon them. If they had no strict principle of honesty, they had, at least, so much honour and virtuous pride, as to scorn imputing to others opinions which they openly disavow, and supporting that injurious imputation, by a gross imposition upon their readers. Whether you have not been guilty of something like this in the case of Mr. Mede[e], I leave others to determine. Were we to grant you, that amongst all the adversaries of the demoniac system, there is not one honest man; surely, you will scarce brand the advocates for it as perfect reprobates. Now, amongst these there are some who understand the word demon in the sense in which I explain it. Dr. Pearce,

[e] Letter I. p. 19, note (f)

late

late lord bishop of Rochester, has been universally (and I believe very justly) esteemed a person of singular probity and piety, as well as an able critic, yet he tells us, that Josephus describes demons to be the spirits of *wicked men*, without expressing any dissent from this account of them[f]. The testimony of so great a judge of the Scripture language deserved to be produced on this occasion.

IV. It still remains, that I examine the objections against this notion of possessing

---

[f] See the bishop of Rochester on Mat. viii. 28. His lordship, indeed, in his note on v. 29, refers to Jude v. 6. and is chargeable with inconsistency, unless he thought (as some others have done) that the angels, or messengers there spoken of, had once been men; or, that wicked human spirits had the same expectation of future punishment with the fallen angels, and referred to Jude only in a general view. It is remarkable, that at the very instant that he cites Josephus's account of possessing demons, as denoting human spirits, he calls the demon which (according to the Jewish historian, Antiq. l. viii. c. 2. sect. 5.) Eleazer expelled, *a devil*; though he knew that a wicked human spirit was intended. So little notion does his lordship seem to have had, that either *demon* or *devil*, was the proper name of the prince of fallen angels.

demons,

demons, which you have drawn from the writings of the PRIMITIVE CHRISTIANS.

Here, Sir, you have bestowed much useless pains in proving, what, I imagine, every one allows, that the Fathers asserted (as we have seen several of the heathen philosophers also did) the existence of malignant demons who never belonged to the human species. You cite, with triumph, Justin Martyr[g], Tertullian[h], Clemens Alexandrinus[h], Cyril[i], Theodoret[i], Basil[i], Origen[i], and Ignatius[i]; to whom you might have added many others[k]. But why did you not proceed one step farther, and shew that these superior demons were the evil spirits to whom possessions were referred by the Fathers of the first, second, and third centuries? This you have not done. The primitive Fathers (as well as the Pagans) believed there were various kinds of demons, some of a celestial, others of a terrestrial origin[l]. Some were entirely

[g] Inquiry, p. 200. [h] Ibid. p. 202. [i] Ib. p. 203.
[k] Dissert. on Mir. p. 216, note. p. 223, & seq.
[l] Ita duo genera dæmonum facta sunt; unum cæleste, alterum terrenum. Lactantius, Div. Institut. l. ii. c. 15. p. 174. ed. Dufresnoy.

of human extract, others sprang from the congress of angels with the daughters of men[m]. The assertion of one species of demons did by no means infer a denial of the existence or power of another.

Athenagoras, who flourished in the second century, reckons *the souls of the giants amongst the demons who wander about the world*[n]. Origen believed, that such as were once men might become demons, and even the devil and his angels[o]. And St.

---

[m] Lactantius (ubi supra), and others, taught that the fall of angels consisted in this polluted intercourse between angels and women, which gave birth to a middle order of demons. Qui autem sunt ex his procreati, qui neque angeli, neque homines fuerunt, sed mediam quandam naturam gerentes, &c.

[n] καὶ αἱ τῶν γιγάντων ψυχαὶ, οἱ περὶ τὸν κόσμον εἰσὶ πλανώμενοι, δαίμονες. Athenag. Apol. p. 28. B. In the fragments of the (spurious) book of Enoch, likewise, human unclean souls are reckoned amongst demons. From this book the most ancient Fathers borrowed their opinion of demons; and particularly the notion of demons being the offspring of angels by the daughters of men.

[o] Jerome (epist. lix.) gives this account of Origen: Ita enim cuncta variari dicebat Origines, ut et qui nunc homo est, possit in alio modo dæmon fieri; et qui dæmon est, et negligentius egerit in crassiora corpora

St. Auſtin repreſents Tertullian, as maintaining, that the ſouls of the worſt men become demons after death; and thus acceding to the opinion of Apuleius[p]. Nor do I recollect any of the fathers but Tatian[q], who did not allow that ſome human ſouls became demons, though at the ſame time they maintained that there were other demons beſides.

pora relegetur, i. e. ut homo fiat. Sicque permiſcet omnia, ut de archangelo poſſit diabolus fieri, et rurſus diabolus in angelum revertantur.—Qui verò non fuerint meriti ut per genus hominum revertatur ad priſtinum ſtatum, fierent diaboli et angeli ejus, et peſſimi dæmones. Concerning Origen, See Diſſert. on Mir. p. 227, 228, 229.

[p] Auſtin (l. de hæres. c. 86.) ſays of Tertullian: eum ſenſiſſe animas hominum peſſimas poſt mortem in dæmonas verti, qui ita accederet ad ſententiam Apulei. Concerning Apuleius, ſee above, p. 38, note (*). From the works of Tertullian, which are come down to us, it appears, that he believed that the worſt demons ſprang *from a corrupted ſtock of angels*, who mixed with the daughters of men. Apol. c. xxii. p. 21. Diſſert. on Mir. p. 224.

[q] Tatian's reaſon for not allowing that any human ſouls become demons, was peculiar to himſelf; for he believed that the ſoul of man dies with his body. But his very denying that demons are the ſouls of men, ſhews what opinion others entertained of them.

You commit the same mistake with respect to the Fathers, as you did with respect to some of the heathen philosophers. The former, as well as the latter, might believe in a higher order of demons, and yet not consider them as the authors of possessions. Justin Martyr, for example, speaks of *a prince of evil demons**, (as well as the spurious Trismegist) to whom he applies the names of serpent, satan, and devil; and he, as well as many other Fathers, held demons who were the offspring of angels by women; yet, what has this to do with the question before us? For, not to observe that this mongrel race of demons, which are neither angels nor men, are different from *your's*ʳ, which are all of a celestial

---

* Inquiry, p. 200.

ʳ Though you allow (Inq. p. 200, 201.), that in the opinion of Justin, Athenagoras, Clemens Alexandrinus, Tertullian, Lactantius, and other primitive writers (amongst whom you ought to have specified Irenæus), demons were begotten by angels upon the daughters of men; yet you scruple not to affirm, " that the Fathers all agreed with the primitive church, in the persuasion, that possessing demons were none other than the devil and

a celestial origin; Justin held an order of demons different from both; viz. the souls of the deceased, and to these he referred possessions. *Those persons*, says he, *who are seized and thrown down by the souls of the deceased, are such as* ALL *men agree in calling demoniacs and mad*[s]. You object[t], " that he mentions this only as the opinion of the Heathens, not as his own." Why then does he say, that it was the opinion of *all* men, without making a single exception? That he could not design to except himself, appears from the context: for he there urges the case of the possessed, as a proof of the permanency of the human soul after the dissolution of the body. These observations were made in the *Essay*, but you take no notice of them, and expect us to believe upon your bare word, that Justin is not speaking of what *all*, but of what *some*, thought of demoniacs, in flat

and his angels." *Inq. p.* 205, 206. You have no right to avail yourself of the authority of the fathers here specified, whose demons were different from your's, and from those of other primitive writers.

[s] Essay, p. 48.   [t] Inq. p. 200.

contradiction to your author. In a word, from the express testimony of Justin, it appears, that till the end of the second century, the universal opinion concerning possessing demons was, that they were human spirits[u].

This continued to be the general opinion even so late as the age of Chrysostom. For, though in order to discredit the notion that the souls of those who died by violence became demons, he says, it was entertained by many of *the meaner sort*[x]; yet, when he is speaking more at large

---

[u] Notwithstanding this decisive testimony of Justin, you are pleased (Inq. p. 201.) to call him " *an authority point blank against myself*, with respect to the distinction I make between demons and devils; because I allow (Essay, p. 49.) that he calls the devil a demon." I have all along admitted, that many held different kinds of demons, some of whom were of human, others of a superior, origin. Between these two species there was a real difference. But though the term demon be not appropriated to a human spirit, it was never applied to any other in relation to possessions, in the age of Justin, whose *authority* (to borrow your own expressions) *is point blank against you*.

[x] Essay, p. 50, note, πολλοὶ τῶν ἀφιλεςίφων, κ. τ. λ.

concerning

concerning the converfion of human fouls into demons, without confining himfelf to the fouls here fpecified, he does not limit the opinion to the meaner fort, but rather afcribes it to the multitude[y], or bulk of mankind: and more than thefe cannot be fuppofed to have yielded credit to poffeffions. Plotinus reprefents thofe who pretended to cure difeafes by expelling demons, *as admired only by the vulgar*, while they were defpifed by men of fenfe, who believed, *that all difeafes proceed from natural caufes*[z].

Nor is it difficult to account for the oppofition which Chryfoftom made to the general opinion concerning poffeffing demons. We have had occafion to obferve, that feveral philofophers, the latter Platonifts efpecially, afferted the exiftence of a higher order of demons, than thofe who had once inhabited human bodies[a]. Some of them, and Porphyry in particular,

---

[y] τοῖς πολλοῖς, Effay, p. 52, note.
[z] Ennead. ii. l. ix. cap. 14.
[a] Differt. on Mir. p. 220, note.

went so far as to maintain, in opposition to the general sentiments of mankind, that the more immediate objects of heathen worship were of a rank superior to the human race; and that these demons did sometimes personate the souls of the dead, gods, and genii.[a] Now, was it not natural for those who had been educated in these principles, to preserve an attachment to them after their becoming Christians[b]? Certain it is in fact, that many, even of the earliest christian

---

[a] Dissert. on Mir. p. 220, note.

[b] You say, "the Fathers had much better instructors than those which I am pleased to give them." *Inq. p.* 161. They had, I acknowledge, Moses and the prophets, Christ also and his apostles, for their instructors; nevertheless, they were as liable to be biassed by prejudices as any other persons, and were, in fact, too often biassed by their attachment to the gentile philosophy. From whom but the heathen philosophers did they learn, that demons of the higher order personate the souls of dead men, procure themselves to be worshipped under their names, feast upon the steam of what was offered to them in sacrifice*, and delight in blood and ordure? Was it from the sacred Scriptures that they learned, that demons were the offspring of angels by women? It was from the Jewish rabbies and Gentile philosophers, that they borrowed almost their whole system

christian converts, though they adopted some new opinions, did not immediately lay aside their old ones, but preserved them even in opposition to the warm remonstrances of the apostles[c]. Now, if the Fathers were seriously persuaded, that superior demons personated human spirits on other occasions, it was not unnatural for them to conclude, that they might do the same in the case of possessions.

Many advantages arose from this conduct. Nothing could more effectually disparage the heathen gods, and the prophecies and miracles ascribed to them, than representing those gods as devils. Besides, by referring possessions to this higher class of demons, the Fathers saved the credit of the system of demonology. In your book upon *Redemption* (p. 134, 2d ed.), you acknowledge, that the Fathers had their *defects*, and that *they have taught our modern divines a more judicious knowledge of the doctrines of christianity, than they had themselves.*

[*] Deut. xxxii. 38. imports only *the view* with which libations and sacrifices were offered to the fictitious deities of the Heathens, notwithstanding what you assert, p. 323. Compare 1 Cor. x. 21.

[c] Essay, p. 373, note (r).

christian

christian martyrs. From the earliest ages, an opinion had prevailed, that the souls of such, especially, as suffered a violent death, were converted into demons[d]; and this opinion had preserved its ground in the time of Chrysostom. Now, what could bring a greater reproach upon the martyrs, than the opinion of their quite changing their nature at death, and becoming mischievous spirits? Hence sprang the zeal of Chrysostom to eradicate the notion, that possessing demons were the souls of such persons as suffered a violent death. His warm opposition to this notion is a proof of its general prevalence amongst Christians till the beginning of the fifth century; and proceeded, perhaps, chiefly from motives of policy[e]. He was in a manner forced

[d] Dissert. on Mir. p. 209, and Lucian's Philopseud. p. 346. ed. Amstelodam.

[e] Though St. Chrysostom sometimes (vid. in Matth. Hom. 28. al. 29. tom. vii. p. 336, cited in the Essay, p. 51, note.) argues in general terms against the opinion of the souls of the deceased becoming demons, yet at other times (De Lazaro, conc. ii. tom. I. p. 727, ed. Montfaucon.) he only opposes this opinion as far as

forced into this oppofition to it, in order to remedy the inconveniences arifing from it with refpect to the martyrs.

I have now examined all your objections againſt the opinion concerning poffeffing demons maintained in the Effay; and, I hope, confirmed what is there advanced as it refpected thofe who died a violent death; and feems even to allow, that the fouls of wicked men do become demons: "They are not (fays he) the fouls of thofe who *die* by violence that become demons, but the fouls of thofe who *live* in their fins." But this language you reprefent (Inq. p. 212.) as an eafy figure of fpeech, becaufe Chryfoſtom adds, ὐ τῆς ἐσίας αυτῶν μεταβαλ-λομένης, ἀλλὰ τῆς προαιρέσεως αυτῶν την ἐκείνων μιμεμένης κακίαν, *their nature not being changed, but their choice being to imitate the malice of demons.* St. Chryfoſtom does not here retract what he had faid before, that the fouls of the wicked, not thoſe of martyrs, became demons; but affigns a reafon why this might be true; viz. "the previous difpofition and refolution of the wicked to imitate the maliciousnefs of demons, which could not be imputed to the martyrs." He next obferves, that the Scripture calls thofe the children of the devil, who are like him, and do his works; which ſhews, that men fo eminently good as the martyrs, could not, without a change of nature, become demons or mifchievous fpirits, though wicked men might become fuch without that change.

to shew, that the Heathens, the Jews, the first founders of christianity, and the primitive Christians, were all agreed in considering them as human spirits.

But you represent this as a very useless undertaking. For you say[f], that inasmuch as "these spirits were judged capable of entering the bodies of mankind, you would fain know where the difference lyes, with regard to the argument, between such possessions, and possessions by other evil spirits." Were the reality of possessions to be taken for granted, it would, I allow, be a matter of very little moment, to determine who the possessing spirits were. But as the reality of possessions is the main point in question, it is of great importance to determine, whether the cause to which they are referred, be capable of producing such effects. If the possessing demons spoken of in the New Testament were heathen gods, that is, such human spirits as were thought to become deities; then the Scripture furnishes us with two unanswerable objections

[f] Inquiry, p. 135, see p. 168.

against the reality of their possessions. For the Scripture both asserts the utter impotence of all the heathen gods[g]; and gives such an account of the state of departed[h] spirits, as is absolutely inconsistent with their having any power of entering the bodies of mankind. Both these objections were urged in the Essay; and I have now the satisfaction to find, that the force of one of them is admitted by Dr. Worthington himself. For you treat the notion, of the souls of dead men having power to enter the bodies of others, as the greatest absurdity[i]. You likewise observe[k], that "we read in Scripture of *the spirits in prison*[l]; but we do not read of any human spirits released from the prison of flesh, being suffered to roam at large, and to be made the scourges and tormentors of living mortals."

With regard to the *moral character* of possessing demons, though you knew I ad-

[g] Essay, p. 189, et seq.   [h] Essay, p. 190, 191. and Dissert. on Mir. p. 161.
[i] Inq. p. 171, 172.   [k] Ibid. p. 182.
[l] 1 Pet. iii. 19.

mitted

mitted, *that the New Testament did certainly, on some occasions, by demons, mean evil spirits*ᵐ; yet you reproach me with *seeming*

ᵐ Dissert. on Miracles, p. 207, note (ˢ); to which very note you refer your readers. *Inq. p.* 183. That I meant possessing demons, is plain from the reference to Mat. ix. 34. See *Essay*, p. 58. Nevertheless, you are, I apprehend, much mistaken in affirming, that demon is never used in Scripture but in a bad sense. *Inquiry, p.* 183, 184. Mr. Mede, whom you misrepresent as being of the same opinion with yourself, has fully proved, that in Acts xvii. 18. 1 Cor. x. 21. 1 Tim. iv. 1. Rev. ix. 20. demon is not to be taken for an evil spirit, but according to the theology of the Gentiles, for a deified human soul, p. 634, et seq. But you think that even in Act. xvii. 18. demon could not have a good meaning, because *the heathen philosophers were but ill-disposed towards Christ and his apostles.* Inq. p. 185. It was very natural for you to take it for granted, that men will misrepresent those whom they dislike: but I think it possible that a Heathen might scorn such a practice; especially in a case where the very absurdity of it would prevent its ill effect. Notwithstanding what I have seen in your book, I am still persuaded that this argument is generally conclusive.

You plead, that δεισιδαιμονια *was taken by the Heathens in a good sense, but that, amongst Christians, it was put for impiety.* Inq. p. 134. How then would St. Paul be understood by the Heathens, when in addressing them he styled them δεισιδαιμονεςερους? See Essay, p. 208.

to have a great tenderness for their moral character[n], and even with *seeming to have a* GREAT VENERATION *for them*[o]. Who grants you an indulgence for using such language, it may become you well to consider.—As to several of the *epithets* applied to demons in the Gospels, I still think, that they do not refer to their *personal qualities*, but to the *effects* they were supposed to produce. You suppose that some devils are *deaf* and *dumb*[p]. Have *spiritual* beings *corporeal* organs? And was it revealed to the evangelists, that the devils to whom you refer were deprived of their speech and hearing? Is it not more natural to suppose, that the men said to be possessed by these demons, were thought to be thereby rendered dumb and deaf? That this was really the case, will appear by comparing the evangelists Matthew and Luke together, in the account they give of the same demoniac. Matthew[q] speaks only of the demoniac as being blind and dumb: *There was brought unto Jesus one possessed with a demon* (in the original it is

[n] Inquiry, p. 325.   [o] Ibid. p. 183.   [p] Ib. p. 51, 322.   [q] ch. xii. 22.

a de-

a demoniac [r]*) blind and dumb: and he healed him, insomuch that the blind and dumb both spake and saw.* This man's disorder, as was shewn in the Essay [s], was that species of madness called *melancholy*, which sometimes renders men both blind and dumb, and was anciently ascribed to possession. Accordingly, when the demon was gone out, or his disorder was cured, the man recovered his speech and sight. In Luke we read, *Jesus was casting out a demon; and it was dumb. And it came to pass, when the demon was gone out, the dumb spake*[*]. Explain the language of Luke in conformity to that of Matthew, and his meaning will be, " Jesus was curing a demoniacal disorder, which had rendered the patient dumb. And no sooner was the disorder cured, than the patient recovered his speech." The Cambridge manuscript reads, προσφέρεται αυτῶ δαιμονιζόμενος κωφός. And, indeed, it is self-evident, that Luke is speaking of the effect of the demoniacal disorder

[r] δαιμονιζόμενος.
[s] P. 113—116.
[*] Luke xi. 14.

upon

upon the patient. If the demoniac recovered his speech at this time, he had certainly lost it before.

When demons are called *unclean*, the reason seems to be, that persons under that melancholy and maniacal disorder, of which they were the reputed authors, were continually defiling themselves with objects esteemed by the Jews unclean[t]. But you suppose these spirits were called unclean, as for other reasons, so for this in particular, their *inhabiting a man's belly, and dwelling in that place which is the receptacle of ordure*[u]. You may more easily quote an authority, than produce a good reason, for this opinion, or for that which you next mention[x]; both of which shock common sense and decency too much, to require or bear a refutation. The very filthiness of this part of your work secures it from being exposed as it deserves.

I cannot conclude this letter, without observing farther, that from the principle here contended for; viz. " that possessions

---

[t] Essay, p. 62.   [u] Inquiry, p. 324.   [x] Inq. p. 325.

were referred to human spirits," it cannot be inferred, that I deny the existence of fallen angels, much less that I deny the existence of human souls in a state of separation from the body.

You are pleased to tell the world, "that I have made short work with the devil and his angels; and have done more than all the exorcists put together ever pretended to: that I have laid the devil, and all other evil spirits, banished them out of the world, and in a manner destroyed their very existence[y]." There may be much wit, but indeed, Sir, there is no truth in this language. I have never denied; nor could I, without great absurdity, take upon me to deny, the existence of evil spirits originally of a rank superior to mankind. And, as we are ignorant of the laws of the spiritual world, it would be great presumption to take upon us to determine the sphere of their operation. That they have no dominion over the natural world, which is governed by fixed and invariable laws, is a truth attested in the amplest manner by reason, by re-

---

[y] Ap. to Inq. p. 332.

velation, and by our own experience. But the question is, whether possessions are referred to fallen angels, or to human spirits. To say they are referred to the latter, is by no means to banish the former out of the world. I do not remember, that Mede, or Sykes, or Lardner, were ever charged with, or even suspected of, what you impute to me, and what you might, upon the same grounds, have imputed to them.

But you go farther still, and affirm, that " I seem to be persuaded, that Beelzebub and all other demons are non-entities[z]; and that I have laboured to prove their non-existence and absolute nullity[a]." You add, " that if these demons, or deified human spirits are all annihilated, all other human souls, after they have left the body, may be reduced to nothing." And you ask with seeming concern, *what becomes of the doctrine of a future state*[b]? To the *Essay*, and other writings of the same tendency, you impute the revival and growth

---

[z] Ap. to Inq. p. 332.   [a] Inq. p. 192, see also p. 330.   [b] Inq. p. 192.

of the *Sadducean creed*, that there is neither *angel nor spirit* [c].

But is it impossible for human spirits to exist, unless they are turned into demons? Does not Dr. Worthington himself allow, that the souls of men survive the dissolution of the body; and, at the same time, deny their power of possessing mankind? If the doctrine of the *Essay* favours the Sadducean creed, that of the *Inquiry* does the same. But you say, the author of the Essay has laboured to prove the non-existence and absolute nullity of demons. What he really attempted to prove, is, that those reputed demons to whom possessions were referred, had no more power to produce these effects, than if they had no existence in nature [d]. But at the same time he contends for the reality of a separate state [e], and for the existence of those very spirits which were falsely believed to be changed into demons, of whom St. James speaks under their vulgar denomination, and of whom he says, that they believe and tremble [f].

[c] Inquiry, p. 227.   [d] Strictly speaking, they had no existence at all *as* demons.   [e] Dissert. on Mir. p. 161.   [f] Essay, p. 211.

Nay,

Nay, notwithstanding all the pains you have taken to misrepresent me as Sadducee, you were willing, in case you were charged with this misrepresentation, to provide yourself with a salve, by saying [g], *you persuade yourself, I did not mean to carry my argument so far*, that is, so far as to conclude against the permanency of human souls, after they have left the body: language, which falls far short of what you know to be my avowed opinion, but which nevertheless serves to shew, you did not really believe me to be a favourer of the Sadducean creed, though you were not very unwilling to convey that impression of me to others.

I cannot conclude this letter, though already of too great a length, without taking notice of one farther argument that you have employed to discredit the notion of possessing demons adopted in the Essay; viz. " that taken from its infernal origin." For you tell us, *it could proceed only from the father of lies; and that wicked spirits infuse a belief of it into weak people* [h]. I intended to compliment you upon this notable discovery, till

[g] Inquiry, p. 192.   [h] Inq. p. 206, 209.

I found you modestly gave the honour of it to St. Chrysostom, and very gratefully acknowledged your obligation to him for his *information*[1]. Still, Sir, I congratulate you upon your easy and expeditious method of answering the arguments of your opponents. You have only to call them suggestions of the devil; that is a sufficient refutation. Your opponents, indeed, might take the same method to refute you; but they are under less temptation to do it, and have some regard to their reputation. Perhaps it would be a matter of prudence in you, Sir, to be somewhat cautious how you claim too great a familiarity with the devil, and profess to be let into his secrets, and to know what particular opinions he infuses into the minds of men. You would not be open to the same suspicion, if, whenever you were at a loss to answer the reasonings of your opponents, you cried out with the honest quaker in the like distress, *Oh argument, Oh argument, the Lord rebuke thee!*

I am,
Reverend Sir, &c.

[1] Inquiry, p. 210.

LETTER

LETTER III.

Reverend Sir,

HAVING examined at large your notion of poffeffing demons, I proceed now to confider your explication of *demoniacal poffeffion.*

You call your performance "an impartial inquiry into the *cafe* of the Gofpel demoniacs." But you have taken very little care to ftate their cafe with precifion; and have, I apprehend, much miftaken or mifreprefented it. You had undertaken to produce "inftances from the New Teftament, of the devil's poffeffing men under different names from that of demon[a]." In order to make good this point, you found it neceffary to rank amongft demoniacs, thofe perfons who were not really fuch.

[a] See above, p. 48, and Inq. p. 152, 155—159.

You mention Judas as "an instance that comes fully up to the case in point[b]." Satan, indeed, is said *to enter*[c] Judas; but he was no more a demoniac than Ananias, *whose heart Satan had filled*[d]. A great distinction is to be made between *satanical*

---

[b] Inquiry, p. 92.

[c] You assert, (Inq. p. 95.) "that the devil did *literally* enter into the body of the traytor." I shall leave this assertion to the rebuke of Calvin. On John xiii. 27, he says, Nimis vero insulse delirant, qui diabolum fingunt essentialiter, ut loquuntur, Judam intrasse. Who is not surprised to find you affirming, upon the authority of the most superstitious amongst all the Heathens, that "evil spirits take the opportunity of conveying themselves into men's bodies while they are at their meals;" and confirming this senseless opinion by a misapplication of John xiii. 27? *Inq. p.* 164, 165. The evangelist, in the passage to which you refer, does not say, that satan entered Judas *with* the sop, but *after* it. The delivery of the sop to Judas, was the circumstance that expressly marked him out as the traytor, and exposed him to public disgrace; and this fired his resentment to such a degree, that he could bear the place no longer. Finding that his treachery was discovered, he thought that he might as well go and receive the reward of it. In this manner, it is not improbable; and at this time, it is certain, the *temptation* of satan gained full *admission* into his heart.

[d] Acts v. 3.

temptation

temptation and *demoniacal poſſeſſion*. Nay, you do yourſelf admit[e], "that many may be too much in the power of the devil, without being bodily poſſeſſed by him."

Nor was the woman[e] whom *ſatan* or the adverſary had *bound*, a demoniac; whether her infirm habit of body proceeded from the relaxation of her nerves, or was *inflicted* by an evil ſpirit. This caſe was explained in the Eſſay[g]; and is, in effect, given up by yourſelf. For you ſay[h], "this caſe, in ſtrictneſs of ſpeech, cannot perhaps be called *a poſſeſſion* ſo properly as an *obſeſſion*. It would, perhaps, have been more proper to have obſerved, that the miracle performed upon her, is not ſaid to conſiſt either in the ejection or repulſion of a demon, but in *making her ſtraight*[i].

The language of Peter to which you next appeal[k], *Jeſus healed all that were oppreſſed of the devil*[l], muſt not be explained by modern opinions, but by the ſentiments of the ancient Jews, who conſidered all diſ-

[e] Inq. p. 156.   [g] Eſſay, p. 76—78.
[h] Inquiry, p. 89.   [i] Luke xiii. 13.   [k] Inq. p. 156.   [l] Acts x. 38. See Eſſay, p. 74.

eaſes,

cases, especially those of the most malignant nature, as proceeding from the agency of some spiritual being[m], acting as the instrument of divine providence[n]. But the Jews did not consider all that were oppressed by an evil spirit or diseased, as being possessed by demons. Nor will you affirm, that all the subjects of Christ's healing power were demoniacs. It is absurd to restrain the language of the apostle to any one particular species of disorders, it being his immediate design to shew, that Christ demonstrated his divine commission, by *healing* (as St. Matthew[o] speaks) *all manner of sickness, and all manner of disease amongst*

[m] See Essay, p. 76. Lightfoot on Luke xiii. 11, 16. and Hammond on John vii. 20.

[n] Non enim invenies Deum ullum opus fecisse, nisi per manus alicujus angeli, Maimonides, Mor. Nevoc. p. 200. We have seen, that, originally, the term *satan*, (which is equivalent to that of *devil*) when applied to an angel, did not express the malignity of his disposition, but the nature of his commission, or his being appointed to act as an adversary. It is probable, however, that the Jews might consider the angel of affliction and punishment as an evil being, but still as acting by divine commission.

[o] Ch. iv. 23.

the people. In this sense the language of St. Peter is understood by our best interpreters[p]. And had you, Sir, when you explained it of such as were possessed by the devil, recollected your own idea of possessions, as not necessarily importing any bodily disease, you could not have been guilty of so great an absurdity as that of making the sacred hstiorian say, what, in effect, you do make him say, that Christ healed all who had no disease to be healed.

No less absurd is it to suppose[q], that St. Paul refers to what the ancients understood by possession, when he tells the Ephesians[r], *In time past ye walked, according to the prince of the power of the air,* the prince and leader of that *spirit* or temper *that now worketh in the children of disobedience.* St. Paul is here describing the state of the unconverted Gentiles, and you suppose that he represents them all as demoniacs[s], though nothing

---

[p] Omnes ægri, qui ad Christum adducuntur, dicuntur insideri a dæmoniis. Hammond on John vii. 20. ed. Clerici.   [q] Inq. p. 158.   [r] Chap. ii. 2.

[s] This strange mistake, I suppose, led you (Inq. p. 204.) to conclude, from the custom of the converts from

thing could be more foreign from his purpose[t].

I have now examined, as I had before promised, all the cases that you have produced, as instances of the devil's possessing men under different names from that of demon; and they serve only to shew, how little you understood your subject. If the doctrine of the learned author, whom you cite with approbation[u], be true, " that *dreaming* is but *possession* in sleep;" there is scarce a man you meet with, who is not possessed. But what has this to do with the demoniacs of the Gospel?

The ancients, both Heathens and Jews, affixed as precise and determinate an idea

---

from Heathenism to renounce the devil at their baptism, and from the ceremony of exorcising the devil which preceded it, that the possessing demons were, in the opinion of the primitive Christians, the devil and his angels. But these renunciations and exorcisms have not the least relation to demoniacal possession. They did not suppose the catechumen or convert to be mad, but to be wicked, and as such under the power of the devil, previous to his baptism.

[t] This passage is explained at large. Dissert. on Miracles, p. 155—161. [u] Appendix to Inq. p. 344

to demoniacal poffeffion, as they did to blindnefs, deafnefs, fevers, palfies, or any other diftemper. And the demoniacs of the New Teftament are the very fame with thofe mentioned in other authors[x]. Both the Syrophenician woman, who was a Heathen, and the evangelifts defcribe the cafe of her daughter in the fame terms[y]. The cafe alfo of the epileptic youth is reprefented no otherwife by the evangelifts, than it is by his father, who was a Jew[z]. It would be as unreafonable to affirm, that the blind, the lame, and the deaf, who were cured by Chrift, were different from thofe defcribed under thefe terms in other countries, as to affirm this concerning demoniacs. Accordingly the facred writers, no lefs than the ancient Jews and Heathens, diftinguifh demoniacs from thofe who laboured under other complaints[a]. Now, wherein did this difference confift? By what fymptoms were they diftinguifhed?

[x] Effay, p. 142. [y] Mat. xv. 22. Mark vii. 25.
[z] Compare Mat. xvii. 15, 18, 19. Mark ix. 17—29. Luke ix. 37—42. [a] Mat. iv. 24. Mark i. 34. Luke vii. 21. ch. viii. 2.

You all along confider demoniacs as perfons who had a demon or devil in them: but this is a very defective account of them; it is not a fufficient difcrimination of them, even on your own principles. For you fuppofe, that evil fpirits enter men with their food, in order to refrefh themfelves with the ordure of the human body. But no one who had a fpirit within him for fuch a purpofe, was, properly fpeaking, a demoniac.

You fometimes fpeak of demoniacs as *great and enormous finners.* In thefe fevere terms you reproach Mary Magdalen[b]. You reprefent demoniacs in general, as *being much more under the dominion of the devil than others*[c]; and fay, that *the end of all diabolical poffeffion muft have been to corrupt the hearts of men*[d]. What you have advanced on this point, is totally deftitute of proof. The gofpel never fpeaks of poffeffed perfons in any terms of reproach. We read of one who had been a demoniac

---

[b] Inq. p. 83.   [c] P. 156, 157. compare p. 220, 326.   [d] Inq. p. 96.

from

from his *childhood*[e]; and according to you, there was another, whom our Saviour called *a daughter of Abraham*[f]. Will you deliberately affirm, that either of these persons was a great and enormous sinner? Were we even to allow the truth of what you have advanced, still you have not determined what measure of moral guilt is a certain sign of possession.

Nor have you pointed out any bodily disorders, by which possession might be certainly known and distinguished. You say, indeed, that it cannot be proved, *that any one demoniac had any other madness, or epilepsy, or other complaint, than such as appears to have been actually caused by possession*[g]. And when speaking of the Gadarene demoniacs, you tell us[h], *You cannot discover any insanity in either of them, but what, in the language of the faculty, was symptomatical, and solely effected by the devils that possessed them*. These expressions imply, that insanity and other disorders might be the effect of possession. But,

[e] Mark ix. 21. παιδιόθεν   [f] Luke xiii. 16.
[g] Inq. p. 9.   [h] P. 41.

though

though you speak of *a symptomatical infanity*, yet you have not informed us of any one symptom of that species of infanity, which is effected solely by devils; and consequently leave us at a loss to determine who are to be deemed demoniacs. Nay, of one demoniac you say[i], "it doth not appear that the man was in the least disordered in his senses; and that no such thing is mentioned of him by the evangelists, even as the effect of his possession." So that according to your account of the matter, a man may be possessed who is not mad; and if he be mad, we cannot pronounce him possessed.

You go farther still; and though not unwilling to allow, that evil spirits may take advantage of men's bodily indisposition[k], (just as you suppose they do of men's eating and drinking); yet you expressly affirm[l], *that it does not appear, that these demoniacs*, those spoken of by Matthew[m], *had any natural disorder at all.* You affirm the same of Judas[n], whom you consider as a demoniac, and who certainly

[i] Inq. p. 16. [k] Appendix to Inq. p. 342.
[l] Inq. p. 9.   [m] Ch. iv. 24.   [n] P. 92.

had no diftemper. With refpect to the daughter of the Syro-phenician woman, *you defire it may be obferved, that here is no one diftemper mentioned, as connected with this cafe*[o]. And fpeaking of Mary Magdalene, out of whom our Saviour is faid to have caft feven demons, you fay[p], *We find not a word of any diftemper, much lefs of any complication of diftempers, which fhe laboured under.*

Such is the account you have given of that demoniacal poffeffion which was afferted by the ancients! You have no conception of it's true nature; nor do you point out thofe peculiar fymptoms, on which the ancients founded their belief of it. This error has led you into many others, and affects the very foundation of your fyftem. Had you either confulted the ancients yourfelf, or attended to thofe extracts from them which were laid before you in the work[q] you undertook to refute, you could not have fallen into fuch grofs miftakes on the fubject.

[o] Inquiry, p. 82. [p] Inq. p. 83. [q] Effay, ch. i. fect. 5, 6.

Demoniacs (or, if I may be allowed the expression, *demonized persons*[r]) were such as were thought to have a demon or demons, not only within them, but *inspiring* and *actuating* them; suspending the faculties of their minds, and governing the members of their bodies. The demons were supposed to inform the bodies of the possessed, in the same manner that their own souls did at all other times.

Hence it came to pass, that every thing said or done by the demoniacs, was often ascribed to the in-dwelling demons. Plato[s], if we may credit Clemens Alexandrinus, affirms, that *demoniacs do not use their own dialect or tongue, but that of the demons who have entered into them.* The testimony of Lucian, when stating the common opinion concerning persons possessed, is full to our purpose: *The patient is silent; the demon returns the answer to*

[r] δαιμονιζομενοι.
[s] Apud Clem. Alex. Strom. I. p. 405, Oxon. οἱ την αὐτῶν ὰ φθέγγονται φωνὴν ὐδὲ διάλεκτον, ἀλλὰ την τῶν ὑπεισιόντων δαιμόνων.

the

the questions that are asked[t]. Accordingly Apollonius thus addresses a youth supposed to be possessed: *It is not you that revile me, but the demon*[u]. The reason of this language is explained by what Apollonius adds, *A demon agitates you*[x].

The demoniac himself indeed is sometimes represented as speaking and acting; but it is because he was the organ or instrument of speech and action to the demon by whom he was inspired and actuated. In these different views, what was said or done, was attributed sometimes to the one, and sometimes to the other. Nor is it unusual on other occasions, to refer the same act indifferently, either to the agent, or to the instrument. The demoniac, during the time of his possession, was so entirely out of his own power, and so absolutely under the influence of the demon, that he was not considered as being him-

---

[t] Ὁ μὲν νοσῶν αὐτὸς σιωπᾷ. ὁ δαίμων δὲ ἀποκρίνεται, ἑλληνίζων, ἢ βαρβαρίζων, Lucian Philopseud. p. 337, tom. 2. ed. Amstel. 1687.

[u] ἐ σὺ ταῦτα ἐρήσεις, ἀλλ' ὁ δαίμων, Philostrat. vit. Apollon. p. 157. ed. Olear. Compare Mark i. 23—26.

[x] δαίμων ἐλαύνει σε. Philostrat. ubi supra.

self, but rather as a demon, and was often addressed under that very title[y].

Demoniacs having been educated in the common opinion concerning the nature and reality of possessions, did (as it was natural to suppose they would) frequently fancy themselves to be possessed. Accordingly we find them addressing the spirits that they supposed to be within them[z], and speaking and acting in conformity to the apprehended sentiments and inclinations of those spirits[a]. They either conceived of themselves as being demons; or spoke in the same manner as if they had been such, because they considered themselves as speaking in their name, and under their influence[b].

The peculiar symptoms of demoniacal possession were certain kinds of insanity, such as the ancients could not account for by natural causes[c], and seemed to argue the seizure of the understanding by a male-

[y] Loquere larva. Plautus, Mercator, act. v. sc. iv. v. 20. [z] Essay, p. 251. note (c). [a] Id. ib. note (s). [b] See Essay, p. 250—256. [c] Id. p. 88.

volent

volent demon, who inftigated the unhappy patient to every thing that was extravagant, and injurious to himfelf and others. It has been fhewn [d], that amongft the Greeks, the Latins, the Jews, and other eaftern people [e], infanity was an infeparable effect of poffeffion: that amongft the primitive Chriftians, reputed demoniacs were all mad, melancholy, or epileptic perfons [f]: and

[d] Effay, ch. i. fect. v.

[e] With refpect to the Turcs, the Arabs, and the Perfians, in particular, my learned and worthy friend, Michael Dodfon, Efq. has referred me to the following paffage in Hyde's Rel. Vet. Perf. p. 400, ed. Oxon. 1760, which confirms what is advanced in the Effay: Quod autem infani æftimarentur fancti, non eft mirum, cum omnes vates, tempore vaticinii, fere erant quafi ecftatici: et fane apud Turcas, qui de dictis oraculis nihil unquam audiverunt, etiam hodie, quivis maniacus æftimatur fanctus, quia fpiritu (ut credunt) afflatus et actus: unde fauftum ducitur talis hominis manicam tangere, vel eum tangere, qui eandem tetigerat. Et talis ab eis & Arabibus vocatur—fpiritu obfeffus, a Perfis—dæmoniacus, furens, feu—furens Deo, numine tactus et afflatus, ἔνθεος.

[f] See Effay, p. 126, 127, and the paffage from Lactantius in particular, there cited, which explains the fentiments of the ancient Chriftians, both concerning the demoniacs of their own times, and thofe cured by Chrift,

and that such likewise were all the demoniacs of the New Testament[g]. The symptoms of the latter are the very same with those of the demoniacs described in other ancient writings; and are all maniacal or epileptic.

In some instances, indeed, no particular symptoms are specified; and hence you are forward to conclude, that some demoniacs had no disorder of understanding, nor any distemper whatsoever. But you forget, Sir, that amongst the ancients, no man was thought to be possessed, who was not insane[h]. These two things, possession and insanity, were supposed to bear to each other the relation of cause and effect; and it was from the latter, that men inferred the former[*]. Hence it came to pass, that to be possessed, and to be mad, were used in a great measure as equivalent expressions. So necessarily was the idea of insanity connected with that of possession,

---

Christ. See also Beza, cited in the Essay, p. 342, note (c).

[g] Essay, ch. i. sect. vi.
[h] Essay, p. 78, et seq.
[*] See Philostrat. vit. Appollon. p. 157.

that

that [...]
Ch[...]
ex[...]
the[...]
a[...] to a different
c[...] the evangelists, therefore, call [...] a *demoniac*; or say, *he had a demon*, they by these very terms represent him as mad. Your notion of demoniacs, though it may be countenanced by a few moderns, is one of the most glaring contradictions to the sentiments of the ancients (who certainly best knew their own meaning) I have ever met with. If the demoniacs of the Gospel laboured under no distemper whatsoever, why is it said, that they were *cured*, and *made whole*[i]; and even that they were *cured* or *healed of evil spirits*[k]? This language implies, that

* Essay, p. 84.

[i] Mat. iv. 24. ch. xvii. 18. Luke vi. 18. ch. ix. 42. Act. v. 16. Concerning the daughter of the Syrophenician woman in particular, it is said, she was made whole, Mat. xv. 28. which ill agrees with your observation, (Inq. p. 82.) " that there is no one distemper mentioned, as connected with this case."

[k] Christ *cured many of infirmities, and plagues, and evil spirits*, Luke vii. 21. *Certain women had been healed of evil spirits and infirmities*, ch. viii. 2.

they had some disease, and that the phrase, *evil spirits*, did itself import a species of diseases. And if that species of diseases was not maniacal, why is the cure of it described by a restoration to sanity of mind¹?

You contradict yourself, as well as oppose the truth, in the account you have given of the nature of demoniacal possession. Though, when it served your purpose, you maintain, that some demoniacs *are mentioned without reference to any distemper whatsoever*ᵐ; yet, at other times, your language plainly implies, that demoniacs, as such, were mad: for you represent their cure as consisting in their *being restored to their right mind*ⁿ. When speaking of the drowning of the swine, you say, " that it proceeded from the rage, which the possession *naturally* produced in them°." Now, if possession produces madness naturally; then every person that was possessed was certainly mad; which

¹ Essay, p. 103.
ⁿ Inq. p. 220.
ᵐ Inq. p. 9.
° Inq. p. 30.

is all that we here undertook to prove. The present question does not concern the reality, but the nature and symptoms, of possession. Even supposing possessions to be real, still it must be allowed, that madness was their concomitant and effect.

From hence it appears, that the question between us, is not, *Whether the possessions mentioned in the Gospel are real or imaginary*[p], in your abstracted view of them, or without including those effects which they were always supposed to produce, and which the very terms, *demoniacal seizure* or *possession*, were used to express. The only proper question on this subject, is, " Whether those kinds of insanity which were considered by the ancients, as the symptoms and evidences of demoniacal possession, were truly such; or proceeded from natural causes."

From the foregoing explication of demoniacal possession, we may also learn, upon what ground it was that the ancients distinguished demoniacs from the diseased,

[p] Inquiry, p. 1.

and

and even from lunatics. That the New Testament itself makes such a distinction, I readily admit. The evangelist says[q], *They brought to Jesus all sick people, that were taken with divers diseases and torments, and* (or *even*) *those which were possessed with devils* (in the original they are described by one word[r], which signifies *demoniacs*), *and those which were lunatic, and those that had the palsy.* Hence you[s], Sir, after many others, raise an objection against the doctrine of the Essay, under a mistaken apprehension, that if reputed demoniacs only laboured under natural disorders, there could be no foundation for the distinction made in the Gospel between their case, and that of the other persons specified by St. Matthew.

When possessions were distinguished from diseases; by the latter, the ancients meaned such diseases as affect only the *body*, or imply some disorder in the corporeal system; while the former supposed an

---

[q] Mat. iv. 24. See Essay, p. 64.
[r] δαιμονιζομένους.
[s] Inq. p. 7, & seq.

alienation

alienation of *mind*, such as did not proceed from any disorder in the corporeal system, but from the immediate presence and agency of a demon. This supposed difference in the two cases, is the obvious ground of the distinction originally made between possessions and diseases: a distinction, however, that the New Testament does not always observe. For, it sometimes comprehends possessions under diseases, or speaks of the latter as a distinct species of the former[t].

As to the distinction made between possessions and lunacies, there is no difficulty in accounting for it. Amongst the moderns, indeed, madmen and lunatics are the same; but they were not so amongst the ancients. Both were considered as cases of possession; both likewise were cases of insanity; nevertheless, they were contra-distinguished from each other on account of their different symptoms. By demoniacs, such as were emphatically so called, and without any farther description,

[t] Essay, ch. i. sect. iv. and p. 352.

the ancients always meaned madmen, or possessed madmen. By lunatics they meaned epileptics. The latter denomination expressed the peculiar symptoms of their disorder; the former was given them, because the paroxysms and periods of it were supposed to be regulated by the moon[u]. As the fits of this disorder were ascribed to possession; so the patients were thought to be more subject to the incursion of demons at the changes of the moon, than at any other time[x].

From these circumstances it is evident, that, in the opinion of the ancients, every demoniac was not a lunatic or an epileptic person; though the latter had a demon no less than the former. Their respective disorders were different in their own natures, and attended with different symptoms. The evangelists, therefore, might as reasonably distinguish between demoniacs and lunatics, as the moderns do between madmen and epileptics. The objection we have been considering, frequently as it has been urged, is excuseable only in an English reader; being built

[u] Essay, p. 120, 121.   [x] P. 122.

entirely

entirely on the false supposition, that lunacy had the same meaning affixed to it by the ancients, as it bears in our own language.

I will trespass on your patience one moment longer, for the sake of observing, that the same person might be both a demoniac (or madman) and an epileptic. Such, perhaps, the youth in the gospel was[y]. He was *lunatic and fore vexed*[z]: he was vexed by a demon, or disordered in his mind, as well as subject to epileptic fits. Or the expression may only import, that during these fits, he was violently agitated by demons, or quite outrageous.

I am,
Reverend Sir,
Your's, &c.

[y] Is aut infanus simul erat et epilepticus, quod non raro fit; aut epilepsia ad lunæ circuitus revertente, quod frequentissimum est, laborabat. Mead's Medica Sacra, p. 82. Sæpe enim evenit, ut post longum tempus dementiæ superveniat epilepsia. Sunt enim affines hi morbi, p. 69. See Essay, p. 118—124.

[z] Mat. xvii. 15.

LETTER

Reverend Sir,

THOUGH you had not formed a juft idea of the nature of demoniacal poffeffion, you have fhewn a very fufficient zeal to fupport its *reality*. Your proofs of this point, I now proceed to examine.

You begin with obferving, that *this is a queftion of facts*[a]; that facts *are objects of fenfe, than which there is nothing we are lefs liable to be deceived in*[b]; that they are the *proper fubjects of teftimony*[b]; and that they ought to be received when *properly attefted*[c]. You obferve farther, that if *fuch facts ftand upon the evidence of a divine teftimony; if they are recorded by infpired writers, they have then a fanction above all that is human*[d]. Thefe general principles

[a] Inquiry, p. 2. [b] Ib. [c] P. 3. [d] P. 5.

you

you apply to the case of the New Testament demoniacs; and plead [e], *that the narrations, which we meet with in the gospel, of persons possessed with evil spirits, run in the usual stile of history, as other historical facts are generally related; and that there is not the least intimation given any where, throughout the Scriptures, that they are to be understood otherwise, than as real matters of fact.* You then distinctly examine the several cases of reputed possession related in the historical books of the New Testament, and argue from the respective circumstances of each. But the great argument which you draw from all these cases, is the apprehended testimony of Christ and his apostles to the facts in question. You all along endeavour to shew, that the language of these divine instructors asserts or implies the doctrine of real possessions.

This being the argument which you have most laboured; and on which many others lay the greatest stress; I will examine it with attention and candour. Much

---

[e] Inq. p. 5, 6. see also p. 12, 13.

was

was said in the Essay [f] to shew its weakness, of which you have taken scarce any notice; and I might content myself with desiring you to answer what has been already offered; but the subject will bear farther illustration.

The various expressions used by Christ and his apostles, which seem to you to assert or imply the reality of possessions, may be comprehended under these three divisions. 1. Such as describe the disorder of the demoniacs. The historians affirm, that the people brought to Jesus, and to his apostles, (not those *who were possessed with devils*, but) *demoniacs* [g], and such as were *vexed with unclean spirits*. They tell us, that one person had *seven demons*; another, *a legion* [*]; and a third, *a spirit of*

---

[f] Inq. p. 307—379.

[g] δαιμονιζομένες.

[*] I here speak, as you do, on the supposition that the words (τὸν ἐσχηκότα τὸν λεγεῶνα) *him that had the legion*, in Mark v. 15. are genuine. It ought, however, to be observed, that Dr. Mill is positive, they are an interpolation. Even supposing them to be genuine, the evangelist might only mean, " him who said he had a legion."

Python

Python[i] or *divination*. Concerning the epileptic youth, the evangelists say[k], the *spirit rent him sore, the demon threw him down, and tare* or *convulsed him:* and concerning the Gadarene demoniac, *he was driven of the demon into the wilderness*[l]. 2. Such as describe the cure of the demoniacs. Matthew affirms, that *Jesus cast out spirits with his word*. Christ himself declares, *Behold, I cast out demons!* He commissioned his apostles *to cast out demons*. And the seventy disciples said to Christ, *Lord even demons are subject to us, through thy name*. 3. Besides these seemingly direct assertions of possessions and dispossessions, several other expressions used by Christ or his apostles, are thought strongly to imply the reality of both. The history represents the demons as speaking to Christ or his apostles, and crying with a loud voice; and it represents these founders of christianity as *rebuking the demons, com-*

---

[i] Πυθωνος. Act. xvi. 16.
[k] Mark ix. 22. Luke ix. 42.
[l] Luke viii. 29.

manding them to hold their peace, and to come out.

It is chiefly from these, or other perfectly similar passages, that you draw this important conclusion, that the possessions and dispossessions spoken of in the New Testament, are attested as real facts; and that they ought to be admitted as such, both on account of the natural qualifications of the witnesses, and their authority as inspired and infallible writers [m]. So well satisfied are you with the force of this reasoning, that you say, " you do not know what can *now* be said to invalidate the belief of these possessions [n]."

I will take the liberty, however, of submitting the following particulars to your consideration.

I. The possession and dispossession of demons, as they are explained by you, even supposing them to be real facts, are not, in their own nature, objects of sense; and therefore cannot be supported by the testimony of sense.

That incorporeal beings are neither visible to our eyes of flesh, nor discernible

[m] Inq. p. 117—123.   [n] P. 123.

by any of our corporeal organs, is too evident to require proof. You yourself were aware of this; for you plead[o], *that facts, which are not objects of sense, may notwithstanding be sufficiently attested and ascertained by their effects and circumstances:* and you apply this observation to the case of possessions and dispossessions, which, you affirm, " *might have been visible enough in their effects and consequences*[p]." To render this remark serviceable to your cause, you should inform us, what those effects and consequences are, which ascertain the reality of possessions and dispossessions. This task you have undertaken; but, I apprehend, without any success.

There are, you observe[q], *many phenomena in the material world which escape our senses, the reality of which notwithstanding, is incontrovertible. We cannot see the wind, but we hear the sound of it, and feel its power.* All men believe there is such a meteor as the wind, *because* they hear the

[o] Inq. p. 3. [p] Ib. p. 143, 144.
[q] Inq. p. 144.

found of it, and feel its sensible effects. And all men will believe the reality of possessions, when you point out, with clearness and certainty, such effects of them as equally fall under the notice of their senses. Instead of doing this, you change the state of the question, and immediately add, *If we are to believe nothing about spiritual beings, but what falls under our senses, we must not believe so much as the existence of any of them.* The question was not, whether we may not have sufficient reason to believe the existence and agency of spiritual beings, though they do not fall under the notice of our senses; but whether their possessions did, in their effects and consequences, fall under the notice of our senses.

"No natural distemper," you farther plead^r, "could ever be attended with more dreadful *agonies* than these possessions were." Pray, Sir, inform the world, by what criterion you distinguish agonies produced by demons, from those which proceed from natural causes. You speak of a

^r Inq. p. 145.

variety

variety of symptoms[r] in the several cases of the New Testament demoniacs. But notwithstanding this variety, you have not pointed out one sure symptom of possession.

If you can not give us any sure sign of possession, you must be equally at a loss to furnish us with any sure sign of dispossession. Self-evident as it is, that the *ejection* of a demon from the human body does no more fall under the notice of our senses, than his *entrance* into it, yet you are pleased to say[s], that " there is as much evidence that a demon is expelled, arising from the work itself, as there is from the cure of a disease; the alteration produced being no less discernible in the one, than in the other." Every one knows what sickness and health are, and therefore cannot be ignorant what alteration is made in a sick man, when he recovers his health. But is possession as obvious to our senses as sickness is? You do yourself plead[t], that many demoniacs do not appear to have any

[r] Inq. p. 145. [s] P. 144. [t] Inq. p. 9. See above, p. 96, 97.

natural diforder at all; and you have not hitherto fhewn what other effects are produced by the devil's entrance into any one. How then can you determine what alteration is made in him, when the devil is expelled?

Had I not good reafon then to call difpoffeffions, fuppofing them to be real, *invifible* miracles, and to affert that they cannot furnifh out any *fenfible* and *public proof* of Chrift's power over demons[u]? Neverthelefs, you fay, *thefe are downright affertions againft fact, as abundantly appears from what has been already obferved*[x]. You will be allowed to ufe this language, when you have pointed out the vifible difcriminating effects of difpoffeffion, confidered abftractedly from the cure of a diftemper. Till then, the moft prudent anfwer you can return to what I had urged to fhew, that the bare expulfion of a fpiritual and invifible being from the human body, can carry no conviction to mankind, is to affirm roundly, *that it does not deferve to have any notice to be*

[u] Effay, p. 386—396.   [x] Inq. p. 145, 146.

taken

token of it [y]. This you have affirmed; but I am perfuaded, you were fcarce fatisfied with yourfelf in fo doing. For you do take further notice of what you pretend did not deferve any.

You take no fmall pains to fhew [z], what furely no one will deny, that thofe miracles could not be *invifible*, which were fo *aftonifhing to multitudes*, and which produced *faith* both in the fpectators and in the patients. But this faith and this aftonifhment were not, could not be, produced, by what was not feen, the fuppofed ejection of a demon; but by what was both feen and heard, the inftantaneous cure of madmen, or their reftoration to perfect fanity, at the fovereign command of Chrift. As to the *confeffion* of the devils themfelves, the *dread* and *confufion* they betrayed at Chrift's prefence, and their inftantly, though *reluctantly*, quitting poffeffion; thefe things, which you urge as public proofs of their being difpoffeffed [a], are the very points to be proved. What is

[y] Inq. p. 146. p. 111, 112, 221.   [z] Ib. p. 146—151, and [a] Ib. p. 146.

wanted,

wanted, is, some authentic and sensible evidence, that what you call the confession, confusion and reluctance of devils, was not merely the language of the demoniacs, speaking under the influence of their disorder, and a belief of their having demons in them, or of their being themselves demons. You plead farther, that the demons were *literally incorporated*[b] *with the demoniacs; and by that means the miraculous dispossessions of them became objects of sense.* You, perhaps, know what you meaned, when you spoke (very philosophically, without doubt) of the *literal incorporation of incorporeal beings with a demoniac.* But as you have not attempted to shew, how this incorporation renders the dispossession of demons objects of sense, I need not inquire into your meaning.

You allow, that there are many *counterfeit* possessions[c]: you ought, therefore, to have enabled us, clearly to distinguish between these, and such as are real. This was the more necessary, as you gravely tell us[d], that *the Heathens were misled by the*

[b] Inq. p. 146.   [c] Ib. p. 34, 213.
[d] Appendix to Inq. p. 327.

ignis

ignis fatuus of the demons themselves, to judge concerning them otherwise than they really were in themselves. Men are no match for superior beings; and, therefore, if we are exposed to their delusions in this matter, who can point out the certain discriminating effects of possessions and dispossessions? Who with safety can trust his senses? But as you were under no necessity of incumbering your scheme with this difficulty, I shall take no farther notice of it.

In their own nature, possessions and dispossessions, according to your account of them, are not objects of sense; and, consequently, are not proper subjects of human testimony. Even supposing them to be real facts, no man can pronounce them to be such, upon any evidence, except that of revelation. For as to *reason*, you have quite precluded it; the reality of demoniacal possession *being*, according to you, *no more an object of reason, than musick is to the deaf, or colours to the blind*[e].

The proper inference from hence is, not what you[f] represent it; viz. *that the evan-*

[e] Inq. p. 142.   [f] Ib. p. 143.

gelifts were very idle in attempting to give any testimony concerning the ejection of demons; but that it is absurd to suppose, that they did give their testimony either to possessions or dispossessions, in the sense in which you explain them. They tell us, that they testified only such things as they had *heard* and *seen*[g]. You, on the contrary, make them testify what they neither saw nor heard. It was not even possible, that the evidence of sense should convince them, or any one else, that a man had any demon at all within him; much less that he had precisely *seven* demons, or an entire *legion*. On this ground, therefore, your doctrine could not be received nor recommended by the apostles.

How very foreign from the purpose then is all that you[h], after many others, have urged concerning the character and competency of the witnesses, and their peculiar recommendations, such as their being eyewitnesses of Christ's cure of demoniacs, and their being commissioned by him to perform the same miracle, together with

[g] 1 John i. 1, 2, 3.   [h] Inq. p. 117—123.

Luke's

Luke's profession as a phyſician? Neither did their general character, nor any of the peculiar recommendations of them here ſpecified, make thoſe things objects of ſenſe to them, which were not ſo to other perſons. Nor can I ſee any reaſon to believe, that the apoſtles were better qualified than others, to judge concerning the nature of any of thoſe diſeaſes, which were the ſubjects of their healing power.

But *facts*, you plead, *may ſtand upon the evidence of a divine teſtimony, if they are recorded by inſpired and infallible writers*[i]. By having recourſe to ſupernatural inſpiration, you give up the natural qualifications of the witneſſes. For what occaſion could there be for a miracle to reveal to them facts, of which, without that miracle, they were capable and competent judges? Either the one or the other of theſe points muſt be given up. But, I apprehend, neither can be maintained. Accordingly, I proceed to ſhew,

II. That the reality of poſſeſſions and diſpoſſeſſions neither was, nor could fitly

---

[i] Inquiry, p. 5, 118.

be, established by the authority of Christ and his apostles, considered as inspired and infallible persons.

You, Sir, have not so much as attempted to prove, that their inspiration extended to the knowledge of the secret cause of those symptoms which were denominated possessions. Nevertheless, till you had previously established this point, you had no right to appeal to their inspiration on the present occasion. It is the fault in reasoning that logicians call *begging the question*. You have no more reason to suppose, that the apostles were miraculously enlightened with the knowledge of demoniacal, than with the knowledge of any other, disorders. Why then should you urge their authority more in one case than in the other? There is no sort of evidence from the New Testament, that demoniacal possession, considered as the cause of insanity, was made the subject matter of revelation. It is never taught as a doctrine[k];

---

[k] You yourself say, (Inq. p. 6.) *Matters of doctrine are delivered in the Gospels, as doctrine.* Where is the doctrine of possessions so delivered?

never

never afferted either by Chrift or his apoftles, when they were opening the contents of their commiffion; though they moft faithfully revealed the whole counfel of God. Indeed, it is a fubject never profeffedly treated of; fcarce ever incidentally mentioned, but in relating the diforder and cure of demoniacs.

It is not only groundlefs, but abfurd, to fuppofe that poffeffions, in the view in which we are here confidering them, were made the fubject matter of revelation. For the miracles performed upon the demoniacs, like thofe performed upon other perfons, were defigned for the conviction, not of believers, but unbelievers. They do not *fuppofe* faith in the authority of Chrift, but *beget* it. Confequently, the nature of thefe miracles is to be judged of by natural reafon alone; not by an authority, which is not admitted previous to their performance. Scarce can you difhonour the firft founders of our religion more, than by making them urge their infpiration and authority, in a cafe to which it could not extend,

extend, and upon perfons by whom it was not yet acknowledged.

These confiderations weigh much with me; and were inlarged upon in the Effay[l]. You have returned no anfwer to them[m]; and till you do, I cannot but be of opinion, that the queftion concerning poffeffions, confidered as a queftion of philofophy, neither is decided, nor could, with propriety, be decided, by the authority of the infpired teachers of chriftianity. This is a fufficient anfwer to your queftion, " Were not the difciples to be trufted with this *efoteric* doctrine?"

From hence it follows, that whatever opinion the evangelifts entertained concerning the reality of poffeffions, is to be

---

[l] Effay, p. 358—363, and p. 363—369.

[m] This is the more remarkable, as (Inq. p. 133.) you quote the words which introduce thefe confiderations. You allow that Chrift and his apoftles had no divine warrant to change the vulgar language, in defcribing the cafe of the demoniacs. But had they any *direct* revelation concerning their real cafe? To fay their language correfponded to what you mean by the *truth of things,* is taking for granted the very point to be proved.

confidered

confidered as their own *private* opinion; in the philofophy of which we have no more concern, than we have in the philofophy of St. Paul, when he faid, *that which thou fowefł is not quickened, except it die*[a]. With the higheſt reverence, let us receive all thofe truths which the meffengers of God have taught us in his name. But it would put an end to many controverfies, were it carefully confidered, that on points not included in their commiffion, thefe meffengers of God have not interpofed their authority; nor can we, therefore, on thefe points, be determined by it.

But if poffeffions and difpoffeffions, according to your abſtracted view of them, are not the fubjects of any teſtimony, whether human or divine; you will naturally afk, how is the language of the New Teſtament concerning them to be underſtood? I anfwer, juſt as the fame language was commonly underſtood in the age in which the Gofpel was publifhed. For

[a] 1 Cor. xv. 36. See Effay, p. 319, 320.

III. The

III. The language of the New Testament relative to possessions, did always imply certain outward and sensible symptoms and effects; it was used principally to express those symptoms and effects; and commonly without any other intention.

1. The language in question did always *imply* certain outward and sensible symptoms and effects. The doctrine of possessions, and the language founded upon it, were not introduced by Christ and his apostles; but had, long before their time, been familiar, as well amongst Gentiles as Jews. By numerous passages from the writings of both, it has been fully shewn, that demoniacal possession, notwithstanding the modern idea you have affixed to this phrase, was anciently thought to produce, and was used to express, some maniacal disorder°. The latter was included in the former: or, in other words, to say of any one, that he had a demon, was to affirm that he was mad. And his being mad, was the sole ground of his being thought to have a

° See above, Letter III. p. 100, et seq. and Essay, ch. i. sect. v. vi.

demon. As poffeffion implied madnefs, fo difpoffeffion implied fanity, or the recovery of the underftanding. If the demon left a man, or the caufe of infanity was removed, the effect ceafed. Not only did the language of the New Teftament relative to poffeffions always imply; but farther,

2. It was, in common life, principally intended to exprefs certain outward and fenfible fymptoms and effects. The direct and immediate intention of every one in ufing it, was to defcribe thefe effects; except in cafes, in which men were profeffedly ftating their opinion on the fubject, and afferting the doctrine of poffeffions.

The New Teftament itfelf will furnifh us with proofs of this point; proofs taken from perfons contemporary with our Saviour, and who lived in Judea, or the countries bordering upon it. A woman who was a Gentile faid to our Saviour, *My daughter is grievoufly vexed with a demon*[p]. A Jew likewife ufed fimilar language, *My fon is*

[p] Mat. xv. 22.

sore vexed, and hath a dumb spirit, and wheresoever the dumb spirit taketh him, he teareth him, and he fometh, and knasheth with his teeth[q]. Now, did either of these persons intend to bear their testimony to possessions, as facts they could ascertain? The language they use was, no doubt, originally built upon the doctrine of real possessions; and they might themselves be of opinion that this doctrine was true; but their direct and immediate design was, to describe those maniacal and epileptic symptoms with which their children were affected: which was all the information they could give to Christ. Now, when the evangelists use the same language, concerning the same persons, affirming concerning one, *that he had an unclean spirit*[r]; and concerning the other, *the spirit tare him, and he fell on the ground, and wallowed foming*[s]; why should not this language, when used by the evangelists, be understood in the same manner as when used by

---

[q] Mat. xvii. 15. Mark ix. 17, 18.
[r] Mark vii. 25. [s] Ch. ix. 20. See Essay, p. 351.

other

other persons; that is, not as a profession of their faith in the reality of possessions, or as an assertion of what they were ignorant of, but as a description of what they did know; namely, those symptoms which were obvious to sense[t]?

If the phrases, *having a demon, being torn* or *convulsed, and thrown on the ground, by a demon,* were directly intended to express certain outward effects; it is reasonable to suppose, that all other similar expressions were used with the like design. That expression in particular concerning

---

[t] When the father of the epileptic youth said, *My son hath a dumb spirit,* could he take upon him to affirm, that the spirit was dumb? His meaning is, that his son was rendered dumb by his disorder. Why then should not the evangelists, when they use the same language, be understood in the same manner? Nevertheless, you make them assert, that some devils are dumb. See above, p. 79. As to the daughter of the woman of Canaan, you ask, *Is it possible to conceive, that all this* (the account of her possession and dispossession) *was no more than a piece of scenery?* You could not have asked such a question, had you considered, that as the woman's intention was to describe the disorder of her daughter, so Christ's intention was to give assurance of her cure.

one demoniac, *he was driven of the demon into the wilderness*[u], must be understood as a description of the effects of his disorder; especially, as the word demon often denotes the disorder itself, without including the cause; as will be shewn in the sequel.

Again, if *having a demon*, be a phrase that was intended to express insanity; having *an unclean, a deaf, a dumb, demon*, or *a spirit of Python*, must have been intended to express different *kinds* or *symptoms* of insanity; especially as we know, that different symptoms of this disorder were ascribed by the ancients to different spirits[x].

For the same reason, having *seven* demons, or a *legion* of them, must have been intended to denote different *degrees*[y] of insanity. Accordingly, we find, in fact, that to have seven demons, was understood both by the ancient Christians, and by the Heathens, as a description of a violent phrensy[z]; and that to be *full demons*, or *ghosts*, was a phrase descriptive of such

[u] Luke viii. 29.   [x] Essay, p. 346, 347, 348.
[y] Essay, p. 348, 349.   [z] See above, Letter I. p. 14, 15.

as were *stark mad*[a]. This observation is made in the Essay, and is a full answer to that question, *Can any one man have a legion of diseases?* though you are pleased to say[b], *I have offered nothing in answer to it.* You had no reason to exclaim[b], *There are not surely six thousand six hundred and sixty-six* KINDS *of madnesses; and I hope the human body, distempered as it is, is not subject to so many distempers of all kinds, as is here implied.* If to misrepresent an author, be the same thing as to answer him; never was any book more compleatly answered than the Essay. Upon the authority of the ancients, I had explained the phraseology of the evangelists, as expressive of different *degrees* of madness; but your objection supposes, that it had been explained of different *kinds* of madness. Concerning the Gadarene demoniac we are told[c], that *many demons*, not many different *sorts* of demons, *were entered into him*, or that he had a *legion*[d] of them: which cannot, therefore, be understood of

[a] Essay, p. 349.   [b] Inq. p. 44.
[c] Luke viii. 30.   [d] Mark v. 15.

the *variety* of his distempers, but of the extreme *violence* of that which he suffered. You tell your readers[e], that "I *pertinaciously* contend, that there had not so much as *one* devil entered into this demoniac;" and add, "Here is a downright and palpable contradiction." To Dr. Worthington, I acknowledge, there is such a contradiction, but not to the sacred writers, who described the disorder of the demoniac, in the language of the age and country in which they lived, without any intention of being understood in a strict and philosophical sense, or of determining the precise number of demons in the person of whom they speak, or of making themselves answerable for there being in him any demon at all. From the very face of the history, it appears, that nothing could be farther from the intention of the evangelists, than to countenance your account of the number of demons in this unhappy man; for they speak of him indifferently, as a person that had *an unclean spirit*, or that *had demons*[f];

[e] Inq. p. 38. [f] See Essay, p. 328.

and

and Chrift commanded only *one* demon to come out. Let Chrift be underftood, as he is by you, according to the letter, and fix thoufand fix hundred and fixty-five devils were left in this patient, after the unclean fpirit was commanded to come out[g].

To thofe who are acquainted with the language of antiquity, it cannot feem ftrange, that various kinds and degrees of infanity fhould be expreffed by terms borrowed from the different nature and number of the demons to whom they were referred; for amongft the ancients nothing was more common, than to call a fuppofed effect by the name of it's apprehended caufe; as will be fhewn in the fequel[h]. In the mean time, I proceed to obferve farther, that,

If the ancients, by demoniacal poffeffion, intended to exprefs infanity; by difpoffeffion, they muft mean the *cure* of that diforder. Sanity being the reputed effect of difpoffeffion; it is natural to fuppofe,

[g] Luke vii. 29. Mark v. 8. Compare Mark i. 23—25.   [h] P. 145.

that they would put the caufe for the effect in this cafe as well as in the former. Accordingly we find in fact, that they did fo. The woman of Canaan who had interceded with Chrift on behalf of her daughter, when fhe returned home, *found the demon gone out, and her daughter laid upon a bed*[j]. What evidence, Sir, had the woman that the demon was gone out of her daughter? Upon your principles, the demon might be ftill lurking within her, for the purpofe you defcribe[k], without doing her any injury. Even fuppofing her daughter to have been really poffeffed, ftill the mother had no evidence of the ejection of the demon from her, but her cure. And what could fhe, with any degree of propriety, be faid to find, but that her daughter was compofed, and in her right mind? This, therefore, muft have been the thing (principally, if not folely) intended, by her finding the demon gone out. It is in the fame fenfe, therefore, that we fhould explain the language of our Saviour to her,

[j] Mark vii. 30.   [k] Inquiry, p. 164.

the demon is gone out of thy daughter [l]. In the very sense here contended for, it is explained by an expositor, to whom you cannot object, I mean the evangelist Matthew [m]: " Her daughter was *made whole* (or *healed* [n]) from that very hour." If the dispossession of demons was not principally intended to express the cure of the demoniacs; why is it said, that Christ *cured many of evil spirits* [o], and that *certain women had been healed of evil spirits* [p].

You ask [q], *Of what disease could it* (the term, *casting out*) *be properly used, where there was no devil to be cast out?* I answer, that from what has been offered above, it appears, that the *ejection* or *casting out* of a demon, though originally adapted to the vulgar opinion concerning real possessions, became expressive of the supposed *effect* of that ejection, the cure of the demoniacs. Nor would you lay so much stress upon this circumstance, did you consider, that the evan-

[l] Mark vii. 29.   [m] Mat. xv. 28.
[n] ἰάθη.
[o] Luke vi. 21.   [p] Ch. viii. 2.
[q] Inquiry. p. 9.

gelists

gelists often use the same language concerning demons, as they do concerning diseases. If it be said of a demon, he is *gone out*[r], it is also said of the leprosy, that it *departed*, or *went from*[s] the leper. And concerning both demons and diseases, men, as we have seen, are alike said to be healed of them. If this be an answer to your objection drawn from the phrase of *casting out* demons in one instance; it is equally an answer to all the instances in which it occurs, though at every turn you are repeating the same objection.

There are other forms of expression concerning demons and those thought to be possessed by them, by which you endeavour to support your hypothesis; but which cannot answer your purpose, any more than those I have already considered. The New Testament represents the demons or evil spirits as speaking, and crying aloud to Christ and his apostles; and the latter as sometimes addressing the former. Hence you infer the reality of possessions[t].

---

[r] ἐξελήλυθε, Mark vii. 29.   [s] ἀπῆλθεν, Mark i. 42.
[t] Inquiry, p. 15.

As

As to the demons addressing Christ or his apostles; this can be understood only of the demoniacs, as I have shewn elsewhere[u]. Demoniacs were thought to be inspired and governed by demons, and to speak and act entirely under their influence[x]. Hence it originally came to pass, that whatever the demoniacs said or did, was referred indifferently to the demon, or to the person said to be possessed by him[y]. When it was referred to the former, the instrumentality of the latter was not excluded. It was he who spoke, though he was supposed to speak, not from himself, but under the influence of a demon. Now, if by demons and their possessions, the

[u] Essay, p. 252, 253, 254.   [x] See above, Letter III. p. 98. et seq.

[y] There is not any thing more common in all languages, than to speak of persons as saying and doing, what they cause others to say and do for them. John the Baptist, we are told, *said to Jesus*, what the disciples of John said by his direction, Mat. xi. 2, 3. And Christ said to his apostles, *It is not ye that speak, but the spirit of your Father that speaketh in you*, Mat. x. 20. The disciples of John, however, and the apostles of Christ were subordinate agents in the execution of their respective commissions.

evangelists

evangelifts intended to defcribe the diforder imputed to this caufe, as we have fhewn they did; then by the language and actions which they refer to the demons, they muft intend thofe actions, and that language, which the demoniacs ufed under the influence of their diforder. As to the things fpoken by the demoniacs, which are faid to fuit rather with the character of demons than of madmen; it is to be remembered, that as the demoniacs conceived [z] themfelves to be really poffeffed by demons, and to be nothing more than their organs, they fpeak in their names, and juft as they imagined the demons themfelves would do [a]. And they might fometimes fancy that they were demons themfelves [b]. Hence their dread of Chrift's power, and their intreaties and expoftulations with him [c].

When

[z] See Effay, p. 251, 252.

[a] Effay, ib.   [b] p. 267, and 271, note (º).

[c] Thus in Matthew (ch. viii. 28, 29.) we read, that the demoniacs *cried out*; but when they faid, *What have we to do with thee*, &c. they manifeftly fuppofe themfelves to be demons, or nothing more than their organs of fpeech. See Mark v. 8. Luke viii. 29.

The

When Mark, for example, says[d], *All the demons besought Jesus,* he must mean that the demoniac did this under the paroxysm of his disorder, and in the name of those evil spirits by which he believed himself to be possessed, or with whom he confounded himself. Such an outward supplication as this, the evangelist was able to attest. Farther he could not go, without the warrant of an immediate and miraculous revelation, to which he does not lay any claim.

But not only does the sacred history represent demons as speaking to Christ and his apostles, but also represents the latter as addressing themselves to the former[e]. You ask, *Can it be supposed that our Lord would address the man's distemper, as a real person*[f]? This question has been so often answered,

---

The case of these demoniacs is considered at large, Essay, p. 226, et seq. and will be further animadverted upon when I come to examine your reasonings upon it. A similar case occurs, Mark i. 23. 26. Luke iv. 33.

[d] Mark v. 12.   [e] See above, p. 113.
[f] Inq. p. 15.

answered, that you ought not to have repeated it, without attempting, at least, to shew the insufficiency of former replies[g]. From Christ's addressing demons, *rebuking* them, and issuing forth his *commands* to them, you can no more infer that he considered them as intelligent agents, than you can infer that he regarded the winds and seas, and fevers, as such, because they are said to be *rebuked* by him, and to obey his commands. I add, that there was a peculiar propriety in Christ's addressing the demons, on all those occasions on which such addresses were intended to have an effect upon the demoniacs, who, on the principles explained above, would apply to themselves what was said to the demons, whose organs only they conceived themselves to be. Thus, when the demons were commanded to hold their peace, and forbidden to proclaim Jesus as the Messiah; these commands were intended to silence the demoniacs (for reasons elsewhere[h] explained) and perhaps were even addressed

[g] See Essay, p. 355—358.   [h] Ib. p. 249.

to them; a demon or spirit being sometimes put for the person supposed to be inspired by him*. As to demons being commanded by Christ *to come out*; this language was explained above; and, therefore, I only observe in this place, that the command could be designed only to evince Christ's power and authority to effect that cure, †which was implied in, and expressed by, the expulsion of demons. The people understood the language of Christ in the sense in which it is here explained; for at the sight of the miracles performed upon the demoniacs, they cried out with astonishment, *With authority commandeth he even the unclean spirits, and they do obey him*[i]. What did, or could, raise their astonishment on these occasions, but the *visible* miracle, the instantaneous cure of the demoniacs, together with the sovereign manner in which it was performed. It is the very language they used, when Jesus rebuked and calmed the raging elements, *What manner of man is this, that*

---

* See Essay, p. 252—256, and p. 277, note (*).
† See Essay, p. 357.   [i] Mark i. 27.

even

even the winds and the sea obey him[k]*!* In both these cases alike, the people were struck only with what they heard and saw; this, therefore, is what their language was intended to express[l].

If the several foregoing observations are just, they serve to confirm what was elsewhere[m] offered to prove, that the language of Christ and his apostles relative to possessions and dispossessions, was, in common life, used principally, at least, to describe certain outward symptoms, or the disorder and cure of demoniacs, and not to declare men's speculative opinion on this subject. It may, however, be objected, that, though the language under consideration expressed certain outward symptoms, it included also their apprehended cause. I proceed, therefore, to shew further,

3. That the language of Christ and his apostles relative to demoniacal posses-

---

[k] Mat. viii. 27.

[l] In the same manner, we should explain the language of the Seventy, *Lord, even the demons* (the disorders ascribed to demons) *are subject to us, through thy name,* Luke x. 17.   [m] Essay, p. 339—358.

seſſions, was commonly uſed with no other deſign, than to deſcribe theſe outward ſymptoms; or, in other words, that demoniacal poſſeſſion expreſſed madneſs in general, without including the cauſe of it, and even when it was expreſſly referred to a different cauſe from the agency of demons.

It was obſerved above[n], that it is very common to give to an effect the name of the cauſe to which it is aſcribed. By Ceres, Bacchus, Venus, Minerva, Neptune, the Heathens very frequently meaned corn, wine, pleaſure, wiſdom, the ſea[o]; though they are really the names of the deities that reſpectively preſided over theſe things. Whenever the ſuppoſed cauſe or author of any thing is put for the thing itſelf, the cauſe or author is not included. When Ceres, for example, ſtands for corn, and Bacchus for wine, corn and wine alone are intended[p]. Now, there is juſt the ſame reaſon for deſcribing certain kinds and de-

[n] P. 135. [o] See Cicero de Nat. Deor. l. ii. c. 23. with the note of Davis, No. 4.
[p] Eſſay, p. 342, note ([b]).

grees of insanity by the spirits to whom they were referred.

Accordingly, we find, in fact, that demon (which was the name of those evil spirits who were supposed to cause madness) and demoniacal possession, were used merely to express madness, without taking the cause into the account. Instances of their being so used by the Greeks[q], and also by the Latins[r], were produced in the Essay. The same modes of speaking were familiar amongst the Jews. We are expressly told, that they gave the names of demons to distempers[s]. Josephus (in a passage cited in the Essay, which you were pleased to overlook, as you have almost all those things which stood most in your way) says concerning certain demagogues, that *they persuaded the multitude to be possessed by demons*[t]; when all that he meaned, was,

---

[q] Essay, p. 82, note (ᵃ). Beza, even when defending demoniacal possession, admits, Nam et Græci medici quoddam istiusmodi furoris naturalibus remediis sanabilis genus δαιμονιον vocant. Essay, p. 343.

[r] Essay, p. 324, 325 [s] Id. p. 85, 86.

[t] Δαιμοναν τὸ πλῆθος ἀνέπειθον. Bel. Jud. l. 2. c. 13. §. 4.

"that

"that the people were worked up into *a phrenfy* by the artifices and eloquence of their leaders." This is a clear proof, that in the age and country of the firſt publiſhers of the Goſpel, *poſſeſſion by demons* was uſed to expreſs inſanity, even in caſes in which that inſanity was aſcribed to a different cauſe from poſſeſſion. Demons and demoniacal poſſeſſion having been put for the *effect* they were ſuppoſed to produce, or *that ſpecies of madneſs* which was aſcribed to them, loſt, in time, their original and limited ſignification[u], acquired a larger meaning, and were uſed for madneſs in general; from whatever cauſe it proceeded. Examples of this nature in our own language, muſt occur to every one. *Lunacy*, which at firſt denoted that peculiar kind of phrenfy over which the moon was ſuppoſed to have an influence, is now uſed for phrenfy in general. St. Anthony's fire, and St. Vitus's dance, ſtill expreſs certain diſorders, but without any reference to the ſaints, from whom they

---

[u] Other ſimilar examples may be ſeen. Eſſay, p. 340, et ſeq. the reaſon of which is explained, p. 340, 344.

at firſt borrowed their reſpective denominations.

In what manner then are the terms, demons and demoniacal poſſeſſion, to be underſtood in the New Teſtament? How can their meaning there be aſcertained? I know of no better method of doing it, than by interpreting them agreeably to the common uſe of the ſame terms amongſt the ancients, amongſt the Jews in particular, ſuch as lived in the age in which the Goſpel was publiſhed; and in correſpondence to the known forms of ſpeech in all nations. Interpret the language in queſtion by this rule, and you muſt allow, that the evangeliſts included in it certain outward ſymptoms and effects; that their direct and immediate intention in uſing it, was to deſcribe theſe effects; and that they had no farther intention. It was thus uſed even by thoſe who believed (as Joſephus did) the reality of poſſeſſions. Beſides the reaſonableneſs (I might ſay, the neceſſity) of ſuppoſing, that all writers uſe cuſtomary forms of ſpeaking in their ordinary ſignification; there are three farther reaſons for

for concluding, that the evangelists have done so on the subject before us. For

First of all, there are instances in the New Testament, in which *demons* or *evil spirits*, and *having* or *being possessed by* them, cannot reasonably bear a different interpretation from that here assigned to these expressions. When the Jews reproached John with *having* (or *being possessed by*) *a demon*[x], why should we not understand them in the same sense as we do Josephus in the forementioned passage from him, that is, as designing merely to represent him as a person disordered in his understanding, from whatever cause his disorder might proceed? Their objection against Christ, *He hath a demon, and is mad*[y], ought to be explained in the same manner; the discourses of Christ appearing to them to argue an alienation of mind. Those who thought more favourable of Christ's discourses, replied, *These are not the words*

---

[x] Mat. xi. 18.

[y] John x. 20. On this passage and Mat. xi. 18. see Essay, p. 97, note (n).

of him that hath a demon[z]; meaning hereby, that they obferved in Chrift's difcourfes no figns of a difordered underftanding. To come ftill nearer to our purpofe, when Luke fays, *Jefus was cafting out a demon, and it was dumb*[a]; we muft by demon underftand a *diforder*[b] that was fo called from it's apprehended caufe; unlefs we will reproach the evangelift with teaching (without any divine warrant) that there are dumb fpirits. Befides, this fame evangelift (whofe language, you, Sir[c], after others, contend, *is more correct, as well as more phyfical, than that of the other evangelifts*) tells us more than once[d], that *Chrift cured or healed many of infirmities, and plagues, and evil fpirits.* Would a correct and phyfical writer ufe fuch language, if evil fpirits were not a fpecies of difeafes, as much as infirmities and plagues? Now, if you grant, as I think you muft, that, on fome occafions, the evangelifts certainly do by demons or evil fpirits, mean

[z] John x. 21. [a] Luke xi. 14.
[b] See above, p. 80. [c] Inq. p. 121.
[d] Luke vii. 21. ch. viii. 2.

the

the diseases imputed to them, why may not this be the case on all occasions?

That this is really the case universally, seems to me highly probable from this farther consideration; viz. that in describing the New Testament demoniacs, they are to be considered only as *historians*, whose proper business, and avowed profession and design it was, to relate facts, of which they were competent witnesses, and concerning which all other persons were to judge as well as themselves. Had they assumed the character of professors of science, they might have attempted to account for the secret cause of those distempers which were cured by Christ; or had they professed to have received an immediate revelation from God concerning the reality of possessions, they might have urged the best authority in support of it. But they assume only the character of well-informed and faithful historians; and, therefore, what they attest concerning possessions, can not be considered as a speculation of philosophy, nor as a dictate of inspiration, but merely as a description of outward facts, which fall under the immediate obfervation of our fenfes. The diforder and cure of demoniacs are facts of this kind; and they were, as we have feen, commonly defcribed in the very fame language which the evangelifts employ. If you go farther, and make them affert poffeffions and difpoffeffions, according to your merely modern interpretation of them, you (though without figning it) injure their character as hiftorians, who in the relation of facts are never to exceed the information they profefs[e] to have received.

A third reafon may be affigned for rejecting your interpretation of the cafe of the Gofpel demoniacs, and for afferting mine, viz. the uniform doctrine of the apoftles, and other prophets of God, concerning the utter inability of demons and all the heathen deities, to do either good or harm to mankind. Your account of poffeffions fuppofes their having an amazing power over the bodies and minds of men, together with the fatal exercife of it. On the other hand,

[e] Luke i. 1, 2, 3.

hand, the apostles represent them as *vanity* and *nothing*[f]. And, therefore, by the possession of demon, and their dispossession, they could only mean to describe a certain disorder, and it's cure.

If the several observations that have been offered under this head are just, then the language of Christ and his apostles, on which you build your doctrine, can yield it no manner of support; and the facts which they attest, are very different from those which you wish to establish by their authority. But, in your opinion, the evangelists were very reprehensible, if they are not to be understood in the manner in which you explain them, as asserting the doctrine of real possessions. I proceed, therefore, to shew,

IV. That they might describe the disorder and cure of demoniacs in the popular language, that is, by possessions and dispossessions, without making themselves

[f] Essay, p. 189, et seq. Your objections against this part of the Essay will be considered in a subsequent letter.

answerable

answerable for the hypothesis on which this language was originally founded.

Three reasons incline me to this opinion, exclusive of those already offered under the several foregoing heads, which alone would be sufficient to establish it. For, if the evangelists had neither any natural nor supernatural qualification to attest possessions or dispossessions, in case they are to be understood otherwise than of outward symptoms; and if the very terms themselves were commonly employed merely to describe these symptoms, exclusively of their cause; how can they be answerable for that spurious doctrine which you father upon them? Nevertheless, for the fuller vindication of the evangelists, I shall mention some farther reasons for believing, that they had no intention, by the language they used on the subject before us, to establish the doctrine of possessions.

1. It is customary with all sorts of persons, to speak on many subjects in the popular language, though admitted to have been originally grounded on a false philosophy. Examples of this kind will immediately
occur

occur to your own thoughts; otherwife, you might find them in the Effay[g]. Now, if you can not deny the fact[h], can you affign a good reafon, why the facred writers fhould not ufe the fame kind of liberty as all other perfons do, and adopt cuftomary modes of fpeaking, without any thought of giving their fanction to the opinions to which they owed their rife.

2. Certain it is, in fact, that the facred writers do, in feveral inftances, adopt the popular language, though grounded on opinions now known to be erroneous, without any defign of eftablifhing the truth of thofe opinions. I here affirm no more than what Chriftians of the greateft eminence, both ancient and modern, have admitted[i]; than what you, likewife, do admit,

[g] Effay, p. 315, et feq.

[h] You even admit, that God *has not profeffedly made any difcoveries of nature.* Introduction to The Scripture-Theory of the Earth, p. 2, 3.

[i] To the conceffions of antient or eminent Chriftians on this fubject, taken notice of in the Effay, p. 318, note (h), p. 321, note (p), p. 329, note (c), p. 335, note (t), and p. 338, note (y), I will add two paffages from

admit, even in a work written on purpose to defend the philosophy of Scripture[k]; and than what has been shewn to be true in many remarkable instances[l]. After what

from Jerome. He says, (in Matth. c. xiii.) *It is the custom of the Scriptures, for the historian so to relate the opinion men had of many matters, as at that time those matters were by all people taken to be.* And again, (in Jerem. xxviii.) *There are many things in the holy Scriptures, which are spoken according to the opinion of the time in which they were done, and not according to their reality.*

[k] In the introduction to your *Scripture-Theory*, p. 7, 8, you say, *The Scripture accounts of some phenomena may not always, perhaps, seem reconcilable to our notions of the laws of nature. But this may proceed from our ignorance, or our prejudice; or, at least from a condescension to, and a compliance with, the weakness and poverty of our understandings, and with the notions which we receive from our senses; which often renders it proper, if not necessary, that matters should be expressed according to the system of appearances; as is the general practice at present, though we live in a philosophical age; the popular language being always the best understood; and therefore the most proper concerning subjects incidentally mentioned, and not professedly treated of; where there is no necessity of combating received notions, which are merely speculative, and attended with no ill consequence, moral or natural. But these cases, you add, seldom happens, and where they do, are easily discerned.* I was willing to transcribe this passage at large, as I had cited only a part of it in the title page.

[l] Essay, p. 317—323.

has

has been already offered on this subject, I will only take notice of one instance, which will be sufficient to shew, that your reasoning, if it proved any thing, would prove too much, and conclude against yourself.

It was generally supposed by the ancients, that the earth was placed in the centre of the universe; and that the sun, the planets, and the fixt stars, did all move round the terraqueous globe in twenty-four hours. On the other hand, the true system of the world supposes the diurnal and annual motions of the earth, while the sun rests in the centre of the planets that surround him. Nevertheless, in direct contradiction to this system, the sacred writers assert both the immobility of the earth, and the motion of the sun. *God laid the foundations of the earth, that it should not be moved for ever*[m]. *The sun riseth*[n]; *and goeth down, and hasteth to the place where he arose*[o]: *he cometh forth out of his chamber, his going forth is from the end of heaven, and his cir-*

[m] Pf. civ. 5.   See also Pf. cxix. 90.   Ecclef. i. 4. Pf. xciii. 1.   [n] Gen. xix. 23.
[o] Gen. xv. 12, 17.   Ecclef. i. 5.

cuit unto the ends of it[p]. Many other expressions in Scripture relative to the sun [q], contradict the doctrine of modern philosophers.

Accordingly when this doctrine was published, or rather republished, to the world by Copernicus, and confirmed by others, it provoked the rage of bigotry as much as the antidemoniac system can do. Twice was the famous Galilei charged with heresy, and committed to the prison of the holy office[r], for maintaining that the

---

[p] Pf. xix. 5.   [q] Joſh. x. 12, 13.   2 Kings xx. 10.   If. xxxviii. 8.

[r] Galilei was not released from prison, till he had engaged never to propagate his tenets. So well did the pope relish the doctrine you have endeavoured to revive, (Irenicum, p. 81, 82, 83.) that the right of private judgment *is liable to some restraints and limitations, in the use and result of it; that it may be abridged by lawful authority;* and that *by the very term of it's being private, it must be limited by a man's own private capacity, as an individual; and by the sphere of his own private concerns, in matters which do not affect the publick.* Is not the conduct of the pope in injoining Galilei silence, a just comment upon your doctrine? Could the greatest enemy to the right of private judgment desire more, than that it should be abridged by what he would call *lawful*

the earth was not, and that the sun was; in the centre of the world'; and for contradicting the Scriptures by both these propositions. Pope Urban the eighth, at whose instigation the Copernican tenets were condemned by the Inquisition, might argue in some such manner as you have done in reference to possessions. " Galilei," might his holiness say, " makes the sacred writers both deny what is true, and affirm what is false; *which is the foulest indignity that could be offered them*ᵗ. The Saviour of the world himself asserts it as a fact, *that God causeth his sun to rise*,

lawful authority? Do you suspect the truth of your own tenets, and that they will not bear a strict examination? Why otherwise do you plead for restraining and abridging the right of private judgment? But I would willingly hope, that you can not be such an enemy to all improvements in knowledge, and to every valuable interest of mankind, as your language would lead us to suppose.

ˢ Solem esse in centro mundi, et immobilem motu locali, &c. Terram non esse centrum mundi, nec immobilem. See Salusbury's life of Galilei, l. ii. c. 3. & l. iii. c. 2. §. i. Riccioli's Almagest. l. ix. §. iv. c. 40.

ᵗ Inq. p. 127.

This

This fact is confirmed by the testimony of sense, as well by the authority of an infallible teacher. But Galilei withstands *this plain declaration of a fact*; and, in flat contradiction to Christ, says, *God does not cause the sun to rise.* Now, if Christ represents God as doing, what he *does only in shew, I do not know how he could be vindicated, if he were accused of being no more than a juggling impostor*[u]. If he was mistaken in this instance, how shall we know when we may give him credit? His credit, and that of all the prophets, must *be held sacred and inviolable, for the sake of the great truths they deliver; and which, if impaired in some respects, will be exposed to the like treatment in others*[x]."

Now, Sir, return a just answer to this reasoning of the Pope against Galilei, and you will thereby refute you own reasoning against the author of the Essay. It might, with much reason, I apprehend, be replied to his holiness, "that the prophets of God never received, nor professed to

[u] Inq. p. 127.   [x] Id. 216.

have

have received, any supernatural instruction on any points of philosophy[y]; at least, not on those points, on which they express themselves in conformity to erroneous systems of it: and, consequently, that our judgment on such subjects is not to be determined by their modes of speaking. Nor have these divine messengers *professedly* taught any erroneous principles of philosophy; not even as their own private opinion, though many incidental expressions are accommodated to that false philosophy which prevailed in their time." Now, this, we have seen, is precisely the case with respect to possession. It is not included in the supernatural instruction of the first founders of christianity. Accordingly, they never teach it as a doctrine; nor do they assert it as their own private opinion, though they adopt the vulgar language concerning it.

It might be replied farther to Pope Urban, " that the sacred writers had just the same reason, as all other persons had, for using technical terms, without making

[y] Dr. Worthington, as cited above, p. 155, note (*).

M themselves

themselves anfwerable for the falfe opinions that firſt gave rife to them." Why do proteſtants, who have no faith in popifh faints, as well as papiſts who have, ſtill affirm concerning any one, that he has St. Anthony's fire; or that he has St. Vitus's dance? Why do even thofe phyficians who deny the influence of the moon over the diſtemper called lunacy, neverthelefs, affirm concerning certain patients, that they are *lunatic?* Why do thofe who laugh at the notion of the *incubus* or *nightmare* being an intelligent agent, as well as Dr. Worthington, who very gravely defends it[z], ſtill ufe the terms to exprefs a bodily indifpofition? Wherefore, to this very day, do aſtronomers, that have adopted the fyſtem of Copernicus, fpeak of the fun as *rifing, fetting,* and *moving?* Becaufe in all the inſtances here mentioned, the language correfponds, though not to the truth of things, yet to common conception and outward appearances. Thefe popular modes of fpeech are underſtood to exprefs thofe appearances only; and being ufed only in

[z] Inq. p. 129.

describing

describing them, no one is so absurd as to misconstrue them into assertions or declarations of men's real opinions on the several subjects to which they refer. This again is as just an answer to Dr. Worthington as to pope Urban. To *have a demon*, was a phrase that was as much understood to express an outward effect amongst the ancients, as the phrase, to *have St. Anthony's fire*, is so understood amongst us. The former, therefore, might be used by those who did not believe in the power of demons, with as much propriety, as the latter is by those who do not believe in the power of St. Anthony. You are not to learn any man's system of astronomy or physic, from his describing certain celestial appearances, or bodily distempers, in the language of the vulgar; but from the account he professedly gives of that system. Proceed, Sir, by the same rule in judging of the real sentiments of the apostles on the subject of possession; form your judgment by their professed doctrine concerning demons, not by their descriptions of demoniacs; in which they might,

might, very innocently, adopt the popular language, without defigning to eftablifh the doctrine on which it was originally founded. This they have done on other fubjects: they might, therefore, do it on this. They have done it on all fubjects not included in their commiffion[a].

3. There

[a] Some have thought, that though our Lord might conform to the cuftomary language of his country, in matters of little or no moment, fuch as the true fyftem of aftronomy; yet, that the cafe is widely different with regard to things of *great importance*, fuch as miftaken notions of demons, which are the fources of endlefs and hurtful fuperftitions. To which I anfwer, that *it is impoffible for God*, or thofe infpired by him, *to lie*, on any occafion, or with refpect to any matter whatfoever. And were it poffible, that the fpirit of God fhould become a teacher of falfehood in matters faid to be of fmall importance; who is to judge whether the fubject be of fmall importance or not? Scarce would any two perfons agree in their opinion about it. You fometimes plead, that the vulgar phrafes of the fun's rifing and fetting, &c. have no relation to revealed truths. *Inq. p.* 129. The fame thing is equally true with refpect to the vulgar phrafes concerning poffeffion by human ghofts; except that the latter, literally underftood, are directly repugnant to revelation. You think " the former never had any effect upon morality." *Inq. p.* 129. But the falfe philofophy on

which

3. There is one very peculiar reason for believing, that the founders of christianity did

which they were built, was the occasion of great impiety. It was this false philosophy (which had contrived so many *eccentricks and epicycles*, in order to account for the motions of the heavenly bodies) that gave occasion to that well-known saying of a certain monarch, *If he had been of God's council when he made the heavens, he would have taught him how to have mended his work.* But whether any of the vulgar phrases, and those in particular which respect possession, do relate to religion and morality, (as you suppose, Inq. p. 128, 129.) or do not; the Scriptures do not professedly warrant the philosophy on which they were first founded. You make a distinction between a *few* terms which took their rise from a mistaken philosophy; and *many whole* passages in *four* different authors (Inq. p. 128, 129.). According to this doctrine, a prophet may affirm what is false, if he does it in a *few* terms, not in *many whole* passages; and *four* authors, it seems, must not take the same liberty as a smaller number. But in reality, more than four of the sacred writers, besides the evangelists, have very innocently adopted the popular language on subjects of natural knowledge; and in very many whole passages. Once more, you understand St. Vitus's dance as *a description* only, but demoniacal possessions in the Gospel as *narrations*, Inq. p. 129. But if it be affirmed of one person, that he *has* St. Vitus's dance; and of another, that he *has* a demon; why should not both these affirmations be equally understood as *descriptions* only? In one word, did use the popular language on the subject of possessions, without intending to establish the popular hypothesis concerning it, because it is allowed that they do, at other times, speak both of demons and bodily disorders, in mere conformity to the vulgar opinion concerning them, without designing to give their sanction to it. Our Saviour affirms, that *when the unclean spirit is gone out of a man, he walketh through dry places.* According to your mode of explaining Scripture, " here is a plain narration of a fact, and no intimation given that it is to be understood otherwise." Nevertheless,

---

assign a good reason, why he who declared in the plainest terms, *God causeth his sun to rise,* might not also declare, *I cast out demons.* The authority and testimony of Christ can no more be urged in one case than in the other. To those disposed to urge it in either case, I know of no satisfactory answer but this, that neither was physic nor astronomy any part of his divine commission. The objection I have been considering, proceeds entirely on this absurd supposition, that God ought to interpose, in order to rectify every error of importance. (See Essay, p. 369, 370.) In the present case, however, God has interposed with the desired view; as is shewn in the Essay, p. 370—376; and, consequently, your objection is without foundation.

verthelefs, every one muſt ſee, what Vitringa[b] expreſsly admits, that it is only a *popular* opinion, which, whether true or falſe, equally ſerved the purpoſe of our Saviour; which was, by the caſe of the relapſing demoniac, to illuſtrate the character of the Jewiſh nation. The ſame evangeliſts who affirm, that the people brought to Jeſus *demoniacs*[c], do alſo affirm, and in (what you call) *the uſual ſtile of hiſtory*, that they brought to him *lunatics*[d]. Now this laſt expreſſion does as plainly aſſert, that the perſons to whom it is applied were under the noxious influence of the moon; as the former expreſſion does that the perſons it deſcribes were under the noxious influence of demons. But did the evangeliſts in the former caſe intend to expreſs their own belief of a *lunar* influence over diſeaſes, and to certify to the world ſuch an influence as a fact? Were they ever thought to have any ſuch intention? Without ſo much as inquiring, what their private opinion was, men clearly ſaw (for in this

[b] Eſſay, p. 329, note (c).
[c] δαιμονιζομένος.   [d] σεληνιαζομένος.

caſe,

case, their prejudices did not intervene, they had no favourite hypothesis to support, and therefore they saw clearly) that the evangelists had no other design than to describe, in the common and well-understood phraseology of the age in which they lived, epileptic symptoms, without, perhaps, so much as thinking of the truth or falsehood of that hypothesis upon which the language was originally founded. It is precisely the same with respect to all those expressions which assert or imply the real influence of demons over certain species of insanity.

By this time, I hope, it appears, how inconclusive is all your reasoning in favour of the doctrine of possessions, drawn from the language of Christ and his apostles.

In your laborious examination of the history of the several demoniacs spoken of in the New Testament, you all along take it for granted, that the demoniacal possessions and dispossessions there mentioned, are so many facts, in the sense in which you explain them. Upon these facts, you build your doctrine, which, you think, can not be disproved, till the facts are disproved.

proved*. And in so much haste were you to produce your witnesses, and to display their qualifications, that you did not duely consider what they were able, and intended, to attest. The possessions and dispossessions spoken of in the New Testament, were certainly real facts; but not in the sense which you contend for, as importing the *entrance* of a spiritual and invisible being into the human body, it's *residence* there, and it's *expulsion* thence. Such facts, supposing them to be real, are not objects of sense, and therefore can not be proper subjects of human testimony. Nor could the apostles attest them, in virtue of any supernatural revelation; which neither was, nor could fitly be granted them for such a purpose. Nevertheless, they were perfectly qualified to attest demoniacal possessions and dispossessions, as these terms imported the disorder and cure of demoniacs. In this sense, and in this alone, these terms were used on all occasions similar to those on which the New Testament writers em-

* Inq. p. 139, 140.

ployed

ployed them. And in no other sense could they be employed by these writers. The terms took their rise, indeed, from a false hypothesis; but the apostles, by adopting the terms, can not be considered as making themselves answerable for the hypothesis on which they were built; especially as the former were used exclusively of the latter.

With how little reason then did you reproach the author of the Essay with building upon this principle, that *it is allowable to profess one thing, and believe the contrary*[e]*; and that it is lawful to dissemble the truth, and even to lie for it*[f]? But how do you prove, that this principle may be deduced from my premises? You prudently save yourself that trouble; and undertake a more easy task, that of largely exposing[g], what you were sure no one would attempt to vindicate, the absurdity and profligacy of the principle itself. Here, Sir, you come off with triumph, where you had no adversary, but were only beating the air, and combating a phantom of your own ima-

[e] Inq. p. 124, 126.   [f] Ib. p. 126, 127.
[g] Inq. p. 126, et seq.

gination.

gination. All that I contend for, is no more than what you yourself admit, and what indeed it is not poſſible for any one to deny, that all men, on ſome occaſions, uſe the popular language, though they reject the hypotheſis on which it was built. Might not I then exclaim as you do, "By what canons of criticiſm, by what figure in rhetorick, are any writers to be underſtood in a ſenſe directly contrary to that in which they expreſs themſelves[h]?" If you offer any juſt vindication of yourſelf, you will thereby vindicate me.

With how little reaſon likewiſe do you repreſent me as impeaching the character and credit of Chriſt and his apoſtles[i]? If I have done this, ſo has Dr. Worthington; ſo have all thoſe Chriſtians who adopt the true ſyſtem of the univerſe; and all who allow that in any inſtance, (and there are none who do not allow that in ſeveral inſtances) Chriſt and his apoſtles expreſs

[h] Inq. p. 125. ſee alſo p. 128.

[i] According to you, I do, *in effect, tell the evangeliſts, that they record untruths; and tell Chriſt himſelf, that he did not do the things which he aſſumed to do.* Inq. p. 127.

themſelves

themselves according to common conceptions or outward appearances, and not to the truth of things. Were there any force in your declamation against me, with respect to this matter, it would conclude equally against yourself, and the whole body of Christians, as well ancient as modern. You say, *I must justify them, (Christ and his apostles) in that respect, (in not thinking as they spake and wrote,* on the subject before us*) from the like manner of speaking and writing, used by them, on other occasions ; or by producing somewhat similar to it out of some other grave authors of antiquity :* which you think can not be done, not even out of writers of romances, for even these must be understood as they write[k]. Your argument is built on this false supposition, that those who adopt the popular language grounded on opinions which they believe to be erroneous, are guilty of insincerity, and of speaking differently from what they think. But are you liable to the charge of falsehood, only because you scruple not to say, the sun rises and sets,

---

[k] Inq. p. 140, 141.

though

though you believe it does neither? No, Sir, you use the vulgar language with perfect innocence, because it expresses certain outward appearances; and you have no intention in using it to contradict your philosophical faith. In like manner the evangelists, supposing them to believe, that neither demons nor the moon have any influence over diseases, might, without the least insincerity, represent some persons as demoniacs and lunatics, because this representation was both designed and understood merely as a description of certain outward appearances and effects. Their language on this subject has been justified by the like manner of speaking on other subjects, used both by themselves, and all other persons, by what you allow[1] to be *the general practice at present, though we live in a philosophical age.* Indeed, Sir, it is you who lessen the character and testimony of the apostles; for you suppose them to bear their testimony to facts, which they were neither naturally nor supernaturally qualified to attest. But ac-

[1] See above, p. 156, note (*).

cording to the explication given in the Essay of the facts in question, the testimony of the apostles deserves the highest credit, because they witness only what they were competent judges of, viz. the symptoms and cure of insanity, which fell under the notice of all their senses.

Equally ill supported is another charge which you advance against me and others who differ from you. In the most tragical strains do you complain of us, as *crucifying the Son of God,* and as *abusing his word*[m], and *abusing language* to such a degree, *that we may as well throw our Bibles away*[n]. The language of the Bible, like that of all other ancient books, is not to be explained by the sentiments of the moderns, but by the use of the same language in the age in which those books were written. The former was the course which you have taken, by which you (I will not say, have abused, but) have misinterpreted the Scriptures. The latter course is that which I pursued; and it is the only one

[n] Inq. p. 82.   [m] Ib. p. 128.

that

that can give the natural and genuine sense of the language of the sacred writers.

I will only take notice of one objection more, viz. that Christ, by using the popular language concerning demoniacal possessions, did certainly countenance[o] the popular superstition, which is supposed in the Essay to be a groundless one. *Would he, you ask[p], who was truth itself, give any countenance to a falsehood? Would he confirm, and even heighten it, and that both by word and deed? The thought is impious to the last degree.* In reading your Inquiry, I so often met with declamation, where I expected an argument, that I was not much surprized at the passages last cited. Surely, Sir, no man ever doubted of its being highly impious, to reproach Christ with countenancing and confirming falsehood. It was in order to clear him from such undeserved reproach, that I shewed at large in the Essay, that the use of the popular language concerning demoniacs, does by no means imply an approbation of the doctrine of

[o] Inq. p. 39, 82, 131, 132, 133. [p] P. 82.

possessions,

possessions; and consequently can not give countenance to the superstitions grounded upon that doctrine. It was also shewn [q], that the apostles of Christ have in the most effectual manner subverted the doctrine of demoniacal possessions, and thereby guarded men against those vile superstitions which will for ever attend it, by constantly inculcating this momentous truth, that *demons are nothing in the world.* If you would speak to the point, prove, if you are able, that every one who uses the popular language on any subject, makes himself answerable for the erroneous system on which it is built; prove, also, that the falsehood of possession is not an obvious and necessary consequence of the nullity of demons. When you have done this, I promise to become a convert to your opinion. In the meantime,

I am,
Reverend Sir,
Yours, &c.

[q] Essay, p. 370—376.

Reverend Sir,

WITH your main argument (which was considered in my last letter) you have intermixed other proofs of the reality of demoniacal possessions; which, though they are of inferior moment, I shall not pass over without notice.

You plead, that if the ejection of evil spirits (in the sense in which you explain this matter) had not been real, the Sadducees, when they saw the apostles undertake to effect it, would have declared, that the doctrine of possession *was no more than a vulgar error*[a]. You likewise suppose, that Herod, when he received Christ's message, *I cast out demons*, would have exposed him as a false pretender, had the terms

[a] Inq. p. 98—100.

admitted of two senses, one of which must be false[b]. This objection supposes, that Herod and the Sadduces understood Christ, as you do, that is, as asserting the reality of possessions; and that they were able to demonstrate the falsehood of this opinion. But in truth neither Herod nor the Sadducees could object in the manner you suppose; because there could be no possible doubt about the miracle in question, the cure of demoniacs; nor was there any ambiguity in the terms that described it; for they always expressed a restoration to a state of perfect sanity. On my interpretation, there was no ground for any cavil; on your's, there was room for this unanswerable objection, viz. that Christ and his apostles appealed to an evidence, which is not an object of sense, nor (by your own account[c]) of reason.

You think that even the Pharisees might have charged Jesus with *sham miracles, if he pretended to cast out devils, when he did not*[d]. Again, you mistake the meaning of casting out demons, and urge an ob-

[b] Inquiry, p. 10.   [c] See above, p. 121.
[d] Inq. p. 60.

jection

jection againſt me, which concludes only againſt yourſelf, who place the miracle in the diſlodging of a ſpiritual being from the human body; which any bold impoſtor might pretend to effect. You very juſtly obſerve, that the objection of the Phariſees, that Chriſt caſt out demons by the aſſiſtance of their prince, *is grounded upon a ſuppoſition of the reality of whatever diſpoſſeſſions it is levelled againſt*[e]. But would this have been admitted by the moſt malicious adverſaries of Chriſt, if the diſpoſſeſſions in queſtion had been *inviſible miracles*, as on your principles they certainly were? In this caſe, they would rather queſtion the truth of the miracles, than run into that great abſurdity of referring them to Beelzebub, as the only method they had of invalidating the evidence ariſing from them, conſidered as publick teſtimonies to Chriſt's divine commiſſion.

As to our Saviour's refutation of the calumny of the Phariſees[f], from which you

---

[e] Inq. p. 49, 50.
[f] *If Satan caſt out Satan, &c.* Mat. xii. 25—30. Luke xi. 15—23.

largely argue[g]; you have taken no notice of what has been urged[h] in reply to your argument; viz. "that our Saviour in refuting the Pharisees, was addressing men whom it was more easy to silence than convince; and who did not acknowledge his divine authority; and therefore very properly, and agreeably to his custom on other occasions, argues with them on their principles, and not at all upon his own[i]."

You

[g] Inq. p. 55, 56, 57, 59, 60.

[h] Essay, p. 331, note (¹), and Dissertation on Miracles, p. 388.

[i] You, Sir, admit, (Inq. p. 55.) that Christ, in one of his arguments, reasons with the Pharisees *on their own principles*. If he did so in one argument, why might he not do the same in the others? When he said, *If I by Beelzebub cast out demons, by whom do your sons cast them out?* you allow that he refutes the Pharisees with their own opinion. Why then should you argue from the rest of his answer, and particularly from the parable of the strong man armed, as if he was instructing the Pharisees in his own opinion, not availing himself of theirs? What has been observed above with respect to the Pharisees, serves to shew, how very inconsiderately it has been said, that Christ, instead of refuting their calumny, should have denied the principle upon which it is founded, and told them plainly,

that

You often draw arguments in favour of real poffeffions, from fome circumftances in the cafe of particular demoniacs. Without having recourfe to the interpofition of fome fuperior being, you cannot, it seems, account for their uncommon exertions of ftrength[k]; nor for their knowlege of Jefus as the Meffiah[l]. I will not here repeat what was offered in the Effay to invalidate the force of both thefe arguments, becaufe you have fcarce taken any notice of it[m].

What

that there were no real poffeffions; fince the leaft reflection may ferve to convince us, that the avowed enemies of Chrift, and fuch thefe men were, would not have been determined by his authority.

[k] Inq. p. 33, 107. That extraordinary ftrength which you urge as a proof of poffeffion, the moft eminent of the faculty (whom you advife your readers to confult) have pronounced a *fymptom* of madnefs; as (you well know) was fhewn in the Effay, p. 275, 276. Infanorum funt hæc omnia, Dr. Mead, Medica facra, p. 66. Wetftein on Mat. viii. p. 354, 355.

[l] Inq. p. 20, 108. The knowledge which the demoniacs had of Jefus was accounted for in the Effay, p. 242—249.

[m] Indeed, with regard to the demoniac at Ephefus, you fay, that *as a demoniac he very probably had heard of Paul's curing fuch in the name of Jefus; for which very reafon, the*

What hope can there be of bringing any controverſy to a final period; or what one good end can be anſwered, by your repeating old objections, without either giving them any new force, or ſhewing the inſufficiency of the anſwers that had been returned to them? Had you duely conſidered, that madmen are often diſtinguiſhed by the quickneſs of their conceptions,

---

demon who poſſeſſed him made the man always avoid St. Paul. Inq. p. 109. This is *making* hiſtory, not *explaining* it. With regard to one demoniac, that at Gadara, you tell us, (Inquiry, p. 19, 20.) he ran to Jeſus, becauſe he was poſſeſſed and impelled by the devil; but you think the demoniac at Epheſus was poſſeſſed, becauſe (as you venture to affirm, though the hiſtory tells you the contrary, Act. xvi. 18.) he always avoided Paul. How happy are you in being able to turn every thing to your advantage! As to the Gadarene demoniac, you affirm, " he had *always* lived in deſolate places;" (Inq. p. 20.) in direct contradiction to the evangeliſts, who tell us, his diſorder often left him and returned. See Eſſay, p. 246, and alſo Beza on Luke viii. 29. As to Chriſt's not having been in this country, ſee Eſſay, p. 246. Why might not a Gadarene know Jeſus to be the Meſſiah, as well as the Canaanite upon the coaſt of Tyre? Mat. xv. 22. As to the caſe of the man in the ſynagogue, ſee Eſſay, p. 243—245, to which you have made no reply.

as well as by their bodily ſtrength; that their diſorder is often partial and temporary; and that the paroxyſms of it do not obliterate former opinions and impreſſions; had you attended withal to the particular circumſtances of the goſpel demoniacs, (ſome of whom did not require to be confined) you would have eaſily accounted for their language and behaviour, without having recourſe to any ſupernatural agency.

You lay ſingular ſtreſs upon ſeveral circumſtances in the caſe of the Gadarene demoniac. I will not here ſtate his caſe at large, becauſe this was done in the Eſſay; where I both propoſed the difficulties of the common opinion concerning him as a real demoniac[n]; and attempted to account for his behaviour on the ſuppoſition of his being merely a madman[o], though ſtrongly poſſeſſed with an opinion of his having demons within him. You have taken much pains to vindicate the popular opinion concerning this reputed demoniac; though

[n] Eſſay, p. 259—265.   [o] P. 266—275.

you have taken very little notice of what was urged againſt it. I ſhall make a few remarks on what you have offered; omitting only thoſe particulars which have already been conſidered.

1. It is obvious to remark, that the very attempt to make this man's diſcourſe with Chriſt appear rational, carries abſurdity upon the face of it. It was from a man's talking and acting irrationally, that the ancients concluded that he was poſſeſſed; as appears from the whole current of antiquity. To the numerous proofs of this point adduced in the Eſſay[p], both from heathen writers and from the evangeliſts, I would here add one from Philoſtratus, who aſſigns this reaſon for believing that a certain youth was poſſeſſed, viz. " his laughing at things at which no other perſon laughed, and then ſuddenly crying, without any reaſon for it; his ſpeaking to himſelf, and ſinging[q]." In the ſame author, as was ob-

[p] Eſſay, p. 80, 81, notes ([l m]). p. 93, et ſeq. & p. 346.
[q] ἐγέλα τε γὰρ ἐφ' οἷς οὐδεὶς ἕτερος, καὶ μετέβαλεν ἐς τὸ κλάειν, αἰτίαν οὐκ ἔχων· διελέγετό τε πρὸς ἑαυτὸν, καὶ ᾖδε.

ſerved

served elsewhere^r, a mother being asked, why she thought her son possessed by a demon, replied, " because the demon takes away his understanding." You, Sir, on the contrary, would establish the certainty of demoniacal possession from the opposite principle, a person's speaking the words of truth and soberness. Thus you argue not only with respect to the pythoness, or raving prophetess at Philippi^s, but to the Gadarene demoniac also, of whose insanity

---

^r Essay, p. 93, note (^d).

^s Inquiry, p. 105. In the same place, you say, " that it is a strange proof of insanity, which is fetched from her steady repetition of that which was none other than a great and most indubitable truth: which yet is the only evidence that is hinted at or insinuated, Essay on Demoniacs, p. 107." In no part of the Essay is the truth uttered by the pythoness, represented as any evidence of her insanity; and in the very page to which you refer your readers, two other proofs of it are urged, viz. " her description as a *pythoness*, which expressed the species of her insanity; and *the manner* in which she followed Paul for many days." As to the truth itself which she spoke, it was observed, that it did but ill suit an evil spirit; and does therefore but ill agree with your notion of her being possessed. Concerning this woman's case, see Essay, p. 105, et seq. & p. 348. Dissert. on Miracles, p. 275.

there

there can be no possible doubt[t]. To force a rational construction upon his language and behaviour, is to make him speak and act out of character, and to destroy the evidence of his being a demoniac. Permit me to examine your farther account of him; for he is the main pillar of your cause.

2. You say[u], that "the devil found, that himself alone was not a match for our Saviour,—and therefore was resolved, before he would give up the contest, to try what *numbers* might do,—and whether they could not keep possession of this one man *in spite* of him." Pray, Sir, consider, whether the devil, if he knew our Saviour to be the Son of God, as you say he did[x], and that he acted by the power of the Most High, would be willing to make such an experiment? Could that sagacious spirit possibly be so absurd, as to imagine, that with the assistance of his associates he could be a match for omnipotence? Let such extravagant fictions be left to the poets. For-

---

[t] Essay, p. 103. [u] Inquiry, p. 26.
[x] Inq. p. 17, 20, 22,

give

give me, Sir, if I say, that of all the wild imaginations that ever entered the mind of man, I know not one that, in absurdity, exceeds the supposition, that superior intelligences would, in a direct and formal manner, enter into a contest with the power of their creator, who can annihilate, in a moment, all the creatures he has made[y].

3. Farther, you suppose, that the devil *impelled the man to run and worship Jesus, with intent,—to flatter him into some indulgence towards him*[z]. This supposition very ill agrees with that knowledge of Christ

---

[y] In the Appendix to your Inquiry, p. 319, you say, "the devil contrived to CROUD a whole legion into the body of one man." This remarkable expression puts me in mind of a question formerly debated in the schools, viz. "How many thousand devils can dance upon the point of a needle, without jostling one another?" You, Sir, I imagine, would have determined this very philosophical and edifying question, in favour of those who maintained that only a few thousands could do it. For you suppose, that six thousand six hundred and sixty-six devils, however skilfully arranged, would be *crouded* in the whole body of a man.

[z] Inq. p. 20.

which you afcribe to him. Could he think, that the Son of God was open to the flattery of an infernal fpirit? This flattery of the devil does alfo ill agree with your notion of his having a mind to try what numbers could effect. You fay, *The devil ftrained all his powers, fummoned his forces together,—in order to difpute the poffeffion of this fingle perfon*[a]. Neverthelefs, he neither made any refiftance; nor could, according to your account of him, have any thought of doing it. For you tell us[b], *he knew it was to no purpofe to make any attempts upon the Saviour of the world, having been fo lately foiled by him* in the wildernefs. In a word, his impelling the man to run to Chrift, is very abfurd; for hereby he himfelf knowingly rufhed into the prefence of his judge and avenger, whofe difpleafure, you acknowlege, he had incurred[c], and whofe power, he knew, it would be in vain for him to refift[d].

4. By the *deep*, which the demons befought Jefus that he would not command

---

[a] Appendix, p. 318, 319. [b] Inq. p. 22, & p. 17, 18. [c] Inq. p. 18. [d] Ib. p 22.

them to go out into, you tell us[e], *you are inclined to think, that they meant the sea or lake of Gennesareth adjoining; into which they had some apprehensions of being sentenced.* Here it is natural to ask, had the demons (whom you consider as *bodiless*[f] and *spiritual beings*) any fear of being drowned? Or, had they only (that symptom of one species of insanity in human beings) a hydrophobia, or dread of water? Or, since you tell us they love ordure, did they fear being sentenced into the water, on account of it's cleansing quality? Lastly, since they had such a dread of water, (to whatever cause you ascribe it) why did they, after they had entered the swine, precipitate themselves into that very sea, which they earnestly wished and prayed to avoid[g]? So far

---

[e] Inq, p. 27. [f] Ib. p. 203.

[g] To remove this difficulty, you allege, that *the drowning of the swine was contrary to the intentions of the unclean spirits, to whom it is not ascribed; but that it proceeded from the rage, which the possession naturally produced in them.* Inq. p. 29, 30. But, on your principles, the demons did certainly bring on themselves the evil they deprecated; for the swine had no insanity, but

far am I from being able to discover any marks of superior intelligence in the language and conduct you ascribe to your devils, that I am inclined on this occasion to adopt your language[h] on another, with some variation. *Search Bedlam, and inquire of all the faculty there, whether they ever knew, or heard of any* MAN, *however foolish or mad, that could be paralleled in point of folly and madness, with the* DEVIL; *if your account of him be just.*

5. One thing more I must take notice of, viz. "Your saying that the history of the Gadarene demoniac *opens such discoveries into the world of spirits, as are not to be met but what was solely effected by the devils that possessed them*; agreeably to the account you give of the men, p. 41. Could you avoid this difficulty, your principles would lead you into a greater. For if a *few* demons in each of the swine *naturally* produced such a degree of rage, as the demons themselves could not controul; surely, a whole *legion* of them must *naturally* produce an inconceivably greater and more uncontroulable degree of rage. Consequently, the demoniac in whom the legion was, did not speak and act under the influence of the devils, but of that madness, which was the natural effect of diabolical possession.

[h] Inq. p. 33.

with *elsewhere in holy writ*[i]. But these discoveries, according to your account of them[k], were made by the devil, when he said, *My name is legion;* and our Saviour had no other concern in them, than barely asking the devil his name. *The extraordinary revelation*[l] (as you call it) concerning the number of our spiritual enemies, was contained in the answer. Have you not read, that the devil was *a liar from the beginning?* Do not you yourself, when you want to discredit any opinion, tell the world, that the author of it is the father of lies[m]? Nevertheless, when you like the opinion which he is supposed to teach, then the same father of lies becomes a teacher of truth, and we are required to receive doctrines upon *his* testimony[n].

Indeed,

[i] Ib. p. 32. [k] Ib. p. 24, 25.
[l] Inq. p. 25. [m] See above, p. 85.
[n] P. 334. What was merely the language of the demoniacs, you often speak of as the confession and testimony of the devil: (Inq. p. 25, 102, 113, 114, 115, 279.) And you think *it strange, that men in these days should have the hardiness to cavil at dispossessions, which were attested by the devils themselves,* p. 116. You here both misinterpret

Indeed, Sir, the more I examine the history of the Gadarene demoniac, the more clearly do I discern the absurdity of the popular explication of it; and the more disposed do I become to have recourse to that given in the *Essay*, which may easily be cleared from your objections°. The very circumstances in this history that you

terpret the fact, and appeal to the authority of a person, that neither bore his testimony, nor deserves any credit. Nor are you very consistent with yourself in representing the devil sometimes as attesting dispossessions, and sometimes as endeavouring to persuade men, that there never were any real possessions; Inq. p. 213, 301, 316, 327. You seem to think, that evil spirits were *moved* to bear their testimony to God's messengers, p. 102; and that their confessions were *extorted* from them, p. 113. But neither Christ nor his apostles would ever accept what you call their testimony; and therefore they could not be constrained by God to bear it; as is shewn, Essay, p. 248, 249.

° You think that Christ's answer to the demoniac, *go*, implied no more than *permission*: (Inq. p. 28.) It was a word that expressed Christ's sovereign command, and therefore attended with efficacy. I will transcribe Beza's note on Mat. viii. 31. *Permitte nobis abire,* ἐπίτρεψον ἡμῖν ἀπελθεῖν Vulg. *mitte nos,* i. πέμψον ἡμᾶς, ut etiam apud Marcum scribitur. Ridiculi sunt igitur qui permissionem voluntati opponunt. That there was
no

you and other learned writers urge as proofs of poſſeſſion, are mentioned in the New Teſtament as illuſtrations and evidences of the higheſt degrees of inſanity.

You urge with peculiar triumph the caſe of Simon Magus as a proof of poſſeſſion [p]. The account given of him in Scripture [q] is, that he practiſed the arts of *ſorcery,* and

no agency of evil ſpirits on this occaſion, and that the deſtruction of the ſwine was calculated to correct the falſe notions entertained of demons, was ſhewn, Eſſay, p. 299—303. But you are offended, that the ſwine grew mad, juſt when the demons are ſaid to enter them, Inq. p. 36, 37. The entrance of demons was the very deſcription of their becoming mad. You would have had our Saviour drop a *hint,* that might contribute to the cure of the ſuperſtitious notions of demoniacal poſſeſſions; Inq. p. 39. Would the Gadarenes have *taken* the hint? ſee Eſſay, p. 373, note ([k]). You ſay, *do you not know, that common madmen are obſerved to frequent ſolitary and unclean places, though they are fit habitations for unclean ſpirits*; Inq. p. 43. Demoniacs fancied themſelves to be poſſeſſed by ſuch ſpirits, and acted accordingly; ſee Eſſay, p. 101, note ([t]). Laſtly, you object to Chriſt's holding a converſation with a madman; Inq. p. 39. An obvious reaſon for this was aſſigned; Eſſay, p. 269. But what good reaſon can be given for Chriſt's holding a converſation with 6666 devils?

[p] Inq. p. 100, 101.   [q] Act. viii. 9, 13.

aſtoniſhed

astonished (not, *bewitched*[r]) *the people of Samaria*; but that he himself was *astonished, beholding the* (genuine) *miracles done* by Philip, those in particular wrought upon demoniacs. *That he was conversant with evil spirits,* is affirmed by you, but not by the historian. And even had he been conversant with spirits, it was not with those to whom alone you refer possessions. You yourself tell us[s], " that Simon Magus pretended to fetch up the souls of the *prophets* from the lower regions; and of *children* who had been slain, to assist him in magical arts." You affirm[t], against all reason, that Simon *saw* evil spirits forced out of the bodies of men, in a *publick* manner. For their expulsion is not an object of sight, and can not, therefore, be considered as a *publick* event. If the dispossessions of demons are included in the miracles which Simon *beheld*[u], the historian,

---

[r] ἐξίστατο is rendered, Act. viii. 13. *he wondered*; and ἐξιςῶν in the 9th verse ought to have been rendered in a sense conformable thereto. See Schmidius on the place, and Dissert. on Miracles, p. 274, note.

[s] Inq. p. 210.   [t] Ib. p. 101.   [u] Act. viii. 13.

by dispossessions, must intend facts that were *visible*, that is, the instantaneous and perfect cures of persons described as being possessed.

I have now examined all your arguments in favour of real possessions, drawn from the history of the New Testament demoniacs[x]. To many, without doubt, it must seem very unnecessary, to have examined so distinctly every minute particular. But you, Sir, and others perhaps, will not make this objection; for an author never offers any thing in support of his argument, which he does not think of importance;

---

[x] I forgot to take notice sooner, that you think (Inq. p. 14.) Luke's saying, that the demoniac in the synagogue at Capernaum had a *spirit of an unclean devil (demon)* is much stronger than the expression in Mark, who only says, he had *an unclean spirit*; (Luke iv. 33. Mark i. 23.) *and more cogently evinces the reality of the possession*. It requires more sagacity than I can claim, to discern the force of this reasoning. But if you will consult Mills and Wetstein on Luke iv. 33. you will find that the true reading in this evangelist is, *an unclean demon*. So that your curious criticism falls to the ground. Compare, however, Act. xvi. 16. Rev. xvi. 14. & Inq. p. 189.

and what to some appears too trifling to be answered, others imagine to be unanswerable, and for that reason to be passed over.

Besides your arguments from the history of the demoniacs of the New Testament, you have produced others from different topics: which, together with some other particulars, will be the subject of the concluding letter.

I am,

Reverend Sir,

Your's, &c.

LETTER VI.

Reverend Sir,

BEING unwilling to leave any thing unnoticed, upon which you appear to lay any stress, I shall trouble you with one letter more, in which I shall consider some particulars which could not be properly introduced sooner. They respect the evidence for or against demoniacal possession, from reason, from experience, from tradition, and from revelation.

I. With regard to natural REASON, you do not undertake to produce from thence any proofs of demoniacal possession. On the contrary, you allow, "that the light of nature discovers not the existence of fallen angels[a];" and maintain, that "they are beings too subtil for the eye of reason

---
[a] Appendix to Inq. p. 327.

to have any discernment of [b];" that the reality of possessions " is quite out of the province of reason, and no more an object of it, than musick is to the deaf; and" (what is truly lamentable!) " that our reason, in it's most improved state,—hardly sees the things before it [c]."

It is not very difficult to guess, what made you so forward to abuse reason, if the observation of an eminent prelate be just, " that no man is against reason, till he finds that reason is against him." Several objections from reason against your hypothesis were urged in the Essay [d]; to which you return the following answer, " It is no sign of a good cause, that men fly from revelation, and appeal to reason, *which is so poor a judge of the matter* [e]." Pray, Sir, does every one who appeals to reason, fly from revelation? Do not you appeal to reason, when you represent the notion of human spirits having power to possess mankind, as being *contrary to all rational and natural principles* [f]? Nevertheless, na-

[b] Inq. p. 162. [c] P. 142. [d] P. 150—172.
[e] Inq. p. 143. [f] P. 171.

tural

tural reason leaves us as ignorant of the powers of the human soul in a state of separation from the body, as it does of the powers of fallen angels.

The subject of possessions is not so entirely out of the province of reason, as you saw fit to represent it. For, though it leaves us ignorant of the world of spirits, it brings us acquainted with the material system, and the laws by which it is governed; particularly with those laws which God has imposed upon the human system. Reason shews, that these laws are as steady and invariable, as those of any other part of nature; and consequently are not impeded or controuled in their operation by the agency of evil spirits, in the manner your doctrine supposes. Your doctrine can never be reconciled with that *fixed order* of causes and effects, which prevails throughout the universe. It is also chargeable with this farther contradiction to natural reason, that it supposes the human system to be governed by different laws in different ages; which there is no more reason to believe, than there is to believe the fame concerning the fun, and moon, and all the hoft of heaven. Thofe maniacal and epileptic fymptoms, which, in times of ignorance and fuperftition, were afcribed to demoniacal poffeffion, are common in all ages; and yet are not, in this inlightened age, referred to the fame caufe; no, not even by Dr. Worthington[g]. Can you ferioufly perfuade yourfelf, that the very fame effects proceed in one age from fupernatural, and in another from natural, caufes; according as men are funk in barbarifm or emerge from it? Men may be more or lefs acquainted with the laws of nature, in different periods of time; but the fupreme legiflator and governor of the univerfe is without any variablenefs, or fhadow of turning.

Should you ever come to be better reconciled to reafon, than you appear to be at prefent, I would beg you to weigh the force of the various arguments from reafon[h], fuggefted in the Effay, againft the reality

[g] You, Sir, (in Inq. p. 213, 337, 338.) admit, that in thefe days, we fee no *certain* inftances of poffeffion.
[h] Effay, ch. i. fect. 9.

of poffeffions. I fhall here take notice of one of thofe arguments, becaufe the force of it feems to be, in fome degree, admitted by yourfelf. It was fhewn[i], that thofe diforders of the underftanding formerly imputed to poffeffion, the very alledged fymptoms and proofs of it, proceed from phyfical caufes. Amongft thefe caufes, violence of paffion was particularly fpecified in the Effay[k]. Now, you cite, with approbation[l], an author, who fays, "that thefe diforders of reafon (that is, fuch as he calls the effects of an unnatural occupation by fpirits) appear *after* grief, love, or fome great difappointment, *have difcompofed the brain.*" Here it is very natural to afk, and I hope, Sir, you will excufe the liberty I take in afking you, What occafion is there to have recourfe to an unnatural occupation of fpirits, in order to account for the diforders of reafon, when love, grief, and great difappointments have difcompofed the brain? If it be allowed, that the diforders of reafon *fucceed* thefe paffions and great difappoint-

[i] Effay, p. 159, et feq.　　[k] P. 160.
[l] Inquiry, p. 272, 273.

ments, is it not natural to suppose, that the former were *caused* by the latter? We can never prove that there is any relation between cause and effect, if effects which uniformly succeed the operation of certain causes, are not produced by them. Nor are we ever to admit more causes of things than are necessary to explain the phenomena. However you may dread being brought before the bar of reason, you venture nevertheless to appeal,

II. To Experience. On this you affirm, the demonology of the ancient Heathens and Jews was, in part, grounded[m]. And you strenuously contend, that *the notion of possessions in general could not have sprung from any other source than that of reality*[n].

Pray, Sir, consider what it was the Heathens and Jews experienced, in the case of supposed possessions. They experienced in themselves, or observed in others, maniacal and epileptic symptoms. From whatever cause these symptoms pro-

---

[m] Append. to Inq. p. 327. Inq. p. 79, 80.
[n] Inq. p. 34, 35, 312.

ceeded,

ceeded, their obfervation and experience did not carry them beyond the fymptoms themfelves. It was from thefe alone, that the ancients concluded, that thofe affected with them were poffeffed. Poffeffion, therefore, is not a matter, that they could judge of by their experience. Their opinion of it's reality was a conclufion of their reafon, that very reafon which you decry as a poor judge of thefe matters, or rather as no judge at all, and which is fo blind as hardly to fee the things before it. In your reafonings on this fubject, you are chargeable with the fophifm, which logicians call, *the affignation of a falfe caufe.* Every thing urged by you or others, in order to fhew, that if wicked fpirits had never given any proof of their power, the belief of it could not have prevailed fo generally in the world, has no other foundation than this deceitful argument. The opinion or belief in queftion was, it may be allowed, founded in facts; but in facts that were attributed to a wrong caufe.

If you afk, " How can we account for the prevalence of the notion of demoniacal poffeffions, poseffions, if it had not been founded in truth°?" I anfwer,

Firft, That the mere prevalence of an opinion, though we fhould not be able to account for it, creates no proof, nor even prefumption, of it's truth; as all thofe muft allow, who confider what abfurdities in point of fpeculation, and what ill-grounded relations with refpect to matters of fact, have compofed the creed of the world. Had the Heathens acted rationally, the reality of poffeffions might

---

° You, Sir, of all men living, fhould be the laft to propofe fuch a queftion as this. For you maintain, that the devil infufes into the minds of men a perfuafion, that fome human fpirits poffefs mankind; Inquiry, p. 206, 209. (cited above, p. 85.) Now, if the devil infufes this perfuafion into the minds of men, why may he not alfo infufe a belief of the reality of poffeffions, however groundlefs it may be? Indeed the latter is manifeftly included in the former. You, therefore, have accounted for the belief of poffeffions, without fuppofing it to be founded in experience. And to me it feems lefs unlikely, that the devil fhould infufe a belief of the reality of poffeffions, (in cafe they had been afcribed to him) than that he fhould perfuade men (as you fuppofe he does, Inq. p. 213.) to believe there *never were any real poffeffions at all*; and thereby leffen men's idea of his own power.

have

have been inferred from their general belief of it. But in this, as in a thousand other instances, *they became vain in their imaginations, and their foolish hearts were darkened*[p]. If no opinion could ever obtain amongst mankind, but what was founded in truth, how could error and delusion take place in the world? How came that very opinion which you treat as absurd and monstrous, (viz. that possessing demons were human souls) to prevail amongst the vulgar Heathens and Christians, which you admit it did[q]?

Secondly, It is not altogether impossible to account, in some degree, at least, for the rise and spread of demoniacal possessions amongst the Heathens, from whom it was propagated amongst the Jews. The Heathens deified every part of nature, and supposed every event of life to be under the direction of it's peculiar presiding divinity. Their diseases, in particular, they referred to the agency of their gods. The symptoms of maniacs and epileptics seemed to them to argue, not only some interposition,

[p] Rom. i. 21.   [q] Inquiry, p. 206.

but

but the immediate prefence of a deity, fufpending the exercife of their underftandings, actuating their bodily organs, and urging them to a conduct injurious both to themfelves and others. Thefe fuppofed effects of their power being evil and mifchievous, were afcribed to a malevolent caufe. For the Heathens thought, that from a being perfectly good, nothing but good could proceed; and that the evils in the world proceed from gods effentially evil. Amongft their gods, they ranked the fouls of departed men. Thefe gods, they imagined, were more likely than any others, to intereft themfelves in human affairs; and were difpofed to do mankind either good or harm, according to their refpective characters. To whom then were they fo likely to afcribe poffeffions, as to the fpirits of wicked men? They believed thefe fpirits to be capable of actuating the human fyftem; and the very belief of their power prepared them to expect the difplays of it. They were likewife of opinion, that wicked men carried with them thofe malignant paffions into the other world,

which

which made them delight in the misery of their fellow-creatures here. Hence it probably came to pass, that maniacal disorders were ascribed to the possession of such demons as were of human extract. Recollect, Sir, the weakness of man's reason, the strength of his passions, the creative power of his imagination, (which perpetually mistakes phantoms for realities^r) together with the debasing and inslaving influence of superstition, and the numerous artifices of pagan politicians and priests to impose upon the credulity of the people; and you will scarce wonder at the prevailing belief of the power of evil human spirits; the proofs of which few had the ability to detect, or the inclination to examine, or so much as the courage to suspect.

Notwithstanding the stress you sometimes lay upon the experience, which, in your opinion, mankind had of diabolical possessions, yet you seem to have distrusted

---

^r At enim Pythagoricos mirari oppido solitos, si quis se negaret unquam vidisse dæmonem, satis, ut reor, idoneus auctor est Aristoteles. Apuleius in Apol. Socratis.

the

the force of this argument, when you said, that demons *are too subtil for the eye of reason, to have any discernment of, though somewhat assisted perhaps by a wretched experience of their malignity*[t]. Accordingly, you look out for a new auxiliary, and that is,

III. TRADITION. You allow, " that the notion of demoniacal possessions had long obtained before our Saviour's time[u];" " that it was not peculiar to the Jews, nor particularly grounded upon the jewish Scriptures[x]; and that it had overspread the gentile world[y]." In order to account for the prevalence of this notion, you tell us, " that the demonology of the ancient Heathens was grounded, partly, upon tradition, derived from the fall[z]; and that " the best notions which they had of evil spirits, were drawn from the jewish Scriptures, and those notions much corrupted[a]."

[t] Inq. p. 162.   [u] Id. p. 139.
[x] P. 79.   [y] P. 80, 314.
[z] Appendix to Inquiry, p. 327. In another place (Inq. p. 153.) you say, " The tradition concerning an evil principle undoubtedly originated from him," the devil.
[a] P. 329.

I should

I should not have taken notice of these assertions, which are scarce consistent with one another, and totally destitute of proof, had not many learned writers, as well ancient as modern, maintained that the Heathens derived their notion of rebellious angels from the tradition of some original revelation, or from the jewish Scriptures. We are told, that Plato *learned from the Egyptian mysteries, that God had formerly thrown many bad spirits from heaven, who, ever since, had been the enemies of mankind: that the Pythagorean description of the fall of these spirits resembles that of Scripture: that Pherecydes Syrus speaks of such a fall of demons or spirits; and that Ophioneus was the chief of that army, which rebelled against the supreme being*[b]. A learned modern[c] affirms, " that the giants attempting to scale heaven, is probably the scripture doctrine of satan's rebellion mythologized[d]." Plutarch

[b] Marsilius Ficinus, cited by Crito, v. 1. p. 235.

[c] The author of Crito, p. 265. See also, p. 232, 240.

[d] Eusebius, (Præpar. Ev. l. v. c. iv. p. 186.) and many others maintain, that the history of the giants in

tarch[e] compares perfons in debt to thofe demons of Empedocles, which, he fays, were driven by the anger of the gods, and fell from heaven; than which, fome think, we can not wifh for a clearer defcription of the devil and his angels. Nor is the great Dr. Cudworth[f] fingular in fuppofing, that Titan's being caft from heaven, was nothing elfe, *but the fall of angels poetically mythologized.* Thefe eminent writers fpeak the general fentiments of Chriftians in all ages. Many of the early converts to the Gofpel had a ftrong relifh of the legends of paganifm, and endeavoured to perfuade the Heathens, that the ground of them was explained in Scripture. Succeeding writers have been mifled by their too great deference to the opinion of the ancient Fathers.

Though I feel the weight of thefe great authorities, I fhall, from a fincere defire of

the book of Genefis, gave occafion to the fables of the Heathens concerning the giants fpoken of above.

[e] In lib. περὶ τῦ μὴ δεῖν δανείζεσθαι

[f] Intellectual fyftem, p. 817.

better

better information, take the liberty of proposing the following queries:

1. Is it reasonable[g] to suppose, that superior created intelligences should enter into a formal contest with the omnipotence of their creator, in the manner these pagan histories (literally understood) imply? I do not think that the Heathens considered them in any other light, than as fables or allegories; nor can I discover any good reason for attempting to explain them as real facts.

2. What positive, or even presumptive, evidence is there that the Heathens borrowed their fables concerning evil spirits from the jewish Scriptures? In the New Testament, indeed, repeated reference is made to angels that sinned, and that kept not their first *estate* or *principality*. But the Old Testament contains no account of the fall of angels; much less does it represent them as scaling heaven, and being thrown down from thence. There is not even the most distant reference or allusion to

[g] See above, p. 186, 187.

such an event, in any of the jewish prophets[h]. How then is it possible, that the Heathens should borrow from their writings, opinions which they do not contain? Not to add, that the opinions in question prevailed over the east[i] from the earliest

[h] You do, indeed, suppose (Appendix to Inquiry, p. 227, 228.) that there is some allusion to Satan's being cast down out of heaven, in Is. xiv. 12, 13, 14, and that he is there called *Lucifer*, and *son of the morning*. But when you had not an hypothesis to serve, your good sense led you to explain the prophet, as he had been universally (I believe) explained, till the time of Athanasius. You say (Boyle's Lectures, v. ii. p. 270, 271.) *Heaven is sometimes used symbolically for a place, as by the term, it must be meant to signify, of great elevation and dignity; but yet confined to this earth below. How art thou fallen from heaven, O Lucifer, son of the morning! says the prophet, of the king of Babylon, with regard to his being dethroned from his earthly kingdom.* (Compare Essay, p. 334.) Nay, in the very place; (Appendix to Inquiry, p. 228.) in which you say, that Isaiah alludes to *this catastrophe* (that which befel the angels, when they were cast out of heaven), you acknowlege that *the prophet's thoughts were occupied about other matters*. Why were not your thoughts occupied upon the same subjects as the prophet's were? Why do you avowedly pervert his words?

[i] I say this, on the supposition that some degree of credit is due to the eastern histories. See Holwell's Tracts, v. iii. p. 13, et seq.

ages, long before the publication of the jewish Scriptures.

3. Is it not certain, that the Jews borrowed their demonology from the Heathens? Many proofs of this point were produced in a former letter[k]; to which a thousand more might be added. The evidence of it is so glaring, that it forced from you a confession, that the jewish doctors were, on one occasion, *obliged to the heathen demonology*[l]. If you say, that the demonology of the Heathens, in case it was not borrowed from the jewish Scriptures, might be grounded upon tradition, derived from the fall; I ask once more,

4. What evidence is there of such a tradition? I am far from taking upon me to say, that there was not an early revelation of the rebellion of angels, and their expulsion from heaven. But hitherto, this point has been asserted only, not proved. If you look into the heathen records, you will find no *tradition* of any original revelation with respect to the subject before us. Uncertain as traditional evidence is,

---

[k] P. 43, et seq.   [l] Inquiry, p. 48.

yet your opinion wants even this support amongst the Heathens. Besides, if there had been such a revelation as that you speak of, would it not have been very surprizing, that it should be preserved amongst the idolatrous Heathens, and not noticed at all by Moses, nor by any of the succeeding prophets; though the Israelites were separated from the rest of the world, with the express intention of making them the depositaries of the oracles of God? Till you can support what you have said on the subject of tradition with some degree of evidence, I shall be in danger of regarding it as a mere hypothesis, to which you have recourse from some imagined convenience only. After all, could you prove what you have asserted, concerning the sources from whence the Heathens derived their demonology; what end could this answer? It would neither determine whom the possessing demons were reputed to be, nor establish the reality of their possessions.

IV. You endeavour to support your doctrine of diabolical possessions, by arguments drawn from REVELATION; such parts of it as have not hitherto come under confideration.

I confidered this fubject in the Effay upon the foot of reafon, as well as revelation; but fo far am I from *flying from the latter*, as you[m] mifreprefent me, that I am not unwilling, that our refpective opinions fhould be tried by this fingle teft, and to abide the iffue.

You are pleafed to affirm, that *the denying of diabolical poffeffions ftrikes at the whole œconomy of revealed religion*[n]. Confident affertions, unfupported by proof, do not deferve a refutation. It was obferved in the Effay[o], that poffeffing demons being the fouls of departed men, the denying their power to enter and torment the bodies of the living, could no way affect the doctrine of fallen angels, nor any other doctrine that might be grounded upon it. The queftion before us has no relation to any fpirits but thofe of human extract. And I am perfuaded no judicious advocate for the power of the devil to tempt mankind

---

[m] Inquiry, p. 143.   [n] Ib. p. 135.
[o] Effay, p. 146, 147.

to sin, will rest the proof of it on passages that refer to a subject totally different, the power of demons or heathen deities to deprive men of their reason. The objection is so very wide of the mark, that it seems rather designed to inflame the prejudices, than to convince the judgment, of your readers.

You farther plead, that *the casting out devils* was a *greater and* more *signal* miracle, than *the healing of any disease*[p]." Were we even to allow, (what you can never prove[q]) that the former requires more power than the latter; yet inasmuch as the bare dispossession of a spiritual being is not an object of sense, it can not carry any conviction to mankind; much less equal conviction with the miraculous cure of a disease[r].

When you mention it as a still farther recommendation of dispossessions, in your view of them, that they were miracles performed *upon the souls, as well as the bodies of men*[s]; you forget that the explication of

[p] Inquiry, p. 217.
[r] Essay, 397, 398.
[q] See Essay, p. 396, 397.
[s] Inq. p. 220, 115.

them

them which you reject, suppoſes the *mind* as well as the corporeal ſyſtem, to be reſtored to a ſtate of perfect ſanity.

You ſometimes plead[t], that there was *a peculiar propriety* in the miracle performed upon the demoniacs, according to your explication of it, becauſe Chriſt came into the world, *to deſtroy the works of the devil*[u]. The apoſtle John, whoſe words you cite, refers to works of a very different nature from poſſeſſions; as all interpreters are agreed, and is evident from the ſurrounding context. The immediately foregoing words are theſe: *He that committeth ſin, is of the devil; for the devil ſinneth from the beginning.* Your argument proceeds upon the falſe ſuppoſition, that poſſeſſions were conſidered as the works of the devil; and that they are here referred to by the apoſtle. Is there not an obvious difference between poſſeſſion and temptation, between inſanity and wickedneſs? Are they not conſtantly referred in Scripture to different authors; poſſeſſion, to demons; and ſin or temp-

[t] Inquiry, p. 175, 176.   [u] 1 John iii. 8.

tations,

tations, to the devil? A farther anfwer to your argument is returned in the Effay*, which I fhall not here repeat.

All the boafted advantages of your fcheme of interpretation with refpect to difpoffeffions, feem to me to be imaginary. Nor am I able to fuggeft one good reafon, why any perfon fhould wifh your interpretation to be true. On the contrary, the account you give of difpoffeffions can anfwer no other end, than to expofe thefe miracles to contempt. Your demons are fpirits of a celeftial origin, and yet delight in blood and ordure: how fhocking the idea! And, what is infinitely to be regretted, you do, in effect, put the Saviour of the world upon a level with thofe profane exorcifts, who made a trade of going about, and perfuading filly people that they could caft out demons, without giving any proper proofs of their having this

---

* Effay, p. 386—396, where it is fhewn, that poffeffions furnifh no proof of the power of any evil fpirits; and that difpoffeffions furnifh no proof of Chrift's power over any. There could, therefore, be no propriety in the miracle in queftion, according to your explication of it, even fuppofing the devil to be the author of poffeffions.

ing

power[y]. What proof did Christ give (or could he give) of his having this power, if, as you pretend, demoniacs might have no distemper at all; not even that which was judged to be a necessary evidence of possession? I most sincerely acquit you of all profane *intention*; but were the most profane unbeliever to rack his invention, he could not give us a more ludicrous and absurd view of the subject than you have given.

So far is your interpretation of possessions from promoting the credit of revelation, that it is injurious to it, in all it's most essential articles. I shall specify a few particulars;

1. The fundamental principle of all true religion is, that the world is under the sole government of God[z], that there is no other invisible being who has any power or dominion over the course of nature; and

---

[y] You are very liberal, when you allow, (Inq. p. 106.) that the jewish exorcisms might, in the age before the Gospel, be attended with success. Would God succeed the attempts of superstition, avarice, and imposture? See Essay, p. 412, in the note.

[z] Essay, p. 183, and Dissert. on Miracles, ch. iii. sect. 5.

that

that evil proceeds from the same hand that dispenses good. This is the uniform doctrine of revelation. And if we examine the constitution of the world, we shall soon perceive, that all the parts of it are equally the effects of the divine operation; that they are, with the nicest skill, adjusted to each other, and unite in carrying on one common design: and consequently they must all have one and the same author. Here is a solid foundation for resignation, gratitude, trust, and all those religious affections included in piety towards God. You, Sir, on the other hand, maintain, that good and evil have different authors. For you say in express terms, *that as God is the author of all good, so the devil is the author of all evil*[a]; and *that he is justly to be reckoned the evil principle*[b]. You likewise assert, that God *sometimes gives the devil great power over the elements of air and fire, and other parts of nature; over the brute creation; and likewise over the persons of men*[c]. There has been occasion to observe,

---

[a] Appendix to Inq. p. 233.   [b] P. 233, 306.
[c] P. 307.

ferved, that your notion of evil having a different origin from good, is directly combated by Isaiah^e, when he introduces Jehovah as afferting himself to be equally the author of both. From hence it follows, that the devil can have no proper power over the elements and other parts of nature. Nor can such a power be reconciled with innumerable other passages of Scripture, which represent God as the only sovereign of the world, who alone can controul the operation of natural causes. Your doctrine subverts the very foundation of all trust in God, and resignation to his disposals. It is destructive also of the virtue and happiness of mankind. Under the influence of this very doctrine, the benighted Heathens ascribed their frosts and tempests, their disappointments and diseases, and all the evils of the creation, to a malevolent spirit; and thereby plunged themselves into all the guilt, and all the misery of the most direful superstitions.

2. Your doctrine of real possessions subverts another fundamental principle of re-

[d] Above, p. 34.   [e] If. xlv. 7.

vealed religion, namely, the *nullity* of all the heathen gods, or their absolute inability to do either good or harm to mankind. The prophets of God in all ages, besides asserting the sole dominion of Jehovah over the natural world, expressly taught [f], (what necessarily follows from that assertion) that all the objects of the heathen worship, that is, all demons, were as impotent as the images that represented them. Numerous passages to this purpose, both from the Old and New Testament, were produced in the Dissertation on Miracles [g]: and one passage of the apostle Paul was inlarged upon in the Essay [h]. You have not controverted the meaning of the former; but though it could not serve your purpose at all, you saw fit to dispute the obvious sense of the latter. The passage to which I refer is in Paul's epistle to the Corinthians, *We know that an idol is nothing in the world* [i]. The Essay [k] asserts, that by *an idol*, we are here to understand a

---

[f] Essay, p. 189, 190.
[g] P. 233, et seq.
[h] P. 193, et seq.
[i] 1 Cor. viii. 4.
[k] P. 194.

heathen demon or deity; and supports this opinion by the natural import of the original word¹, and by the undoubted application of it in ancient writers ᵐ, as well as by several very great authorities ⁿ; but more especially by the occasion ᵒ on which it is here used by the apostle. You, Sir, on the contrary maintain, that by *an idol,* we are to understand *the material image.* The first reason you assign for this opinion is ᵖ, that the Corinthians, though they might know, that idols of wood and stone were (as the

---

¹ εἴδωλον. See Le Clerc's Supplement to Hammond on 1 Cor. viii. 4.

ᵐ Essay, p. 194, 195, and Elsner on 1 Cor. viii. 4.

ⁿ Le Clerc, in his Latin version of Stanley's History of Oriental Philosophy, p. 176, after shewing that the Heathens called the ghosts of the dead εἴδωλα; and that the Jews and the Christians applied the term εἴδωλον to the pagan gods themselves, and not to their images only, adds, Hinc videtur etiam Paulus, 1 Cor. viii. 4. dixisse εἴδωλον esse οὐδὲν, idolum esse nihil, hoc est, evanidam umbram. I had referred you to several interpreters in support of this opinion, Essay, p. 194; and yet you scruple not to affirm, that *they* (the commentators) *all* UNANIMOUSLY *suppose, that by the idol is meaned, the material visible image,* Inquiry, p. 196, 197.

ᵒ Essay, p. 196.   ᵖ Inq. p. 193.

apostle

apostle speaks^q) *dumb*, yet they could not know that the gods themselves were dumb. *On the contrary*, you add, *they were often supposed to speak.* The Corinthians in their Gentile state, like other Gentiles, might suppose that their gods spoke and conversed with men; but at their conversion to christianity*, they had been taught, that their former objects of worship were void of all the powers ascribed to them; a sentiment often inculcated by the Old Testament writers^r, in passages which you greatly pervert, when you confine their meaning to the material idol. You could not have fallen into so egregious a mistake, had you considered, that the Heathens themselves were not so absurd, as to believe that merely material images possessed sense and reason, and speech^s: that their belief

---

q 1 Cor. xii. 2.

* That the apostle is here speaking of the knowlege peculiar to Christians, is shewn, Essay, p. 229, et seq.

r Pf. cxxxv. 15. Pf. cxv. 3. Hab. ii. 18.

s Arnobius (adverf. Gent. l. vi.) makes the Heathens say, in their own defence, Neque nos æra, neque auri argentique materias——eas esse per se deos,

belief was, that the gods were brought into thefe images by facred dedication, and kept their refidence there[t]: and that in virtue of their being inhabited by the gods, the images were to be regarded and worfhipped as gods[u]. It is in direct oppofition to this opinion, that the prophets reprefent the heathen idols or gods as mere fenfelefs materials; thefe materials, as they were not really inhabited and animated by any deity, nor indued with any divine power, being the only objects of their worfhip. In this view the reprefentation of the heathen idols or gods as only gold and filver, wood and ftone, and

We do not think brafs and gold and filver, and other materials of images, to be of themfelves gods.

[t] Eos in his colimus, eofque veneramur quos dedicatio infert facra, & fabrilibus efficit habitare fimulachris, fay the Heathens in Arnobius, ubi fupra.

[u] *If idols are nothing,* fays Celfus, (apud Origen. c. Celf. l. viii. p. 393.) *what harm can there be to join in the public feftivals? If they are demons, then it is certain that they are gods, in whom we fhould confide.* You remember that Stilpo was condemned by the Athenians to banifhment, for denying the Minerva of Phidias to be a real divinity. See Gen. xxxi. 19, 30. ch. xxxv. 4. Exod. xxxii. 1. Levit. xix. 4. Dan. v. 4.

the work of men's hands, was forcible and ftriking. But what fenfe is there in affirming concerning a merely material idol, that it is mere matter[x]?

You object to my fpeaking of the heathen demons or deities as nullities, and mifreprefent me as afferting, abfolutely, their non exiftence[y], though I had explained my meaning to be, "*either* that they had no exiftence," (*as* demons they had none) "*or* that they were of no-more account, than if they did not exift[z]." What lefs could the apoftle mean when he faid, " an idol is *nothing* in the world?" You had no occafion therefore to expofe the abfurdity of inferring from this text the non-exiftence either of material images or of human

---

[x] I do not know, why you quoted Chryfoftom, with approbation, (Inq. p. 195, 196.) who, in anfwer to that queftion, *Have graven images no exiftence?* replies, they are only *ftones and demons*; unlefs it was to fhew that he underftood the apoftle in a fenfe different from what you do, and contradicted all the prophets of God, who taught that graven images were not inhabited by demons, nor indued with any fupernatural power.

[y] See above, p. 83.   [z] Effay, p. 224.

spirits.

spirits. Ridicule misapplied always returns upon it's author. After all, you seem to acknowlege every thing that my argument requires, viz. " that the material images were representations of fictitious deities, which in truth are no gods; and equally impotent and insignificant as the images themselves [a]. And you elsewhere allow [b], (what indeed it would be absurd to deny) that the sacred writers, and Paul in particular, do, by the term demon, describe the heathen gods, such as their worshippers took to be deified human spirits [c]. Let us now see how far this consists with a

[a] P. 196.   [b] P. 180, 181.

[c] Hereby, I acknowlege, you contradict yourself: for you most commonly contend, that by demon in the New Testament we are to understand the *devil*, or one of his angels, *Inq. p.* 186. I will not on this occasion adopt your polite language to Dr. Grey, (in your book upon Redemption, p. 403, note). *What must the reader think of a man that thus glaringly contradicts himself, for the sake of cavilling at another?* But I will say, that it is difficult, even for men of learning and ability, when they have adopted a false hypothesis, to be always consistent with themselves in their defence of it.

belief of the reality of demoniacal possession.

If the demons or deities of the Heathens were, as you yourself are forced to allow, *as impotent and insignificant as their images;* then these deities have no more power to enter and torment the bodies of men, and to deprive them of their reason, or, in other words, to possess them, than the images have. Now, is it not a necessary, and most obvious, consequence from hence, that there never was, nor can be, a real demoniac? Had I not reason to affirm, that Christ and his apostles had entirely subverted the doctrine of possessions[d]? Nevertheless, you exclaim, (with due reverence, we must presume,) *Good God! where is this to be seen*[e]*?* I answer, in all those passages of Scripture which assert the utter impotence of all the demons of the Heathens. It was moreover shewn in the Essay, that God's inspired messengers, by establishing the nullity (or if that word offends you, the *nothingness*) of demons, with respect to any power over mankind,

[d] Essay, p. 314. [e] Inquiry, p. 198.

took

took the moſt proper and effectual method of overturning not only the doctrine of poſſeſſions, but all the other ſuperſtitions grounded on the contrary opinion[r]. You have attempted to evade this evidence by ſaying[s], "that poſſeſſions are not ſo properly matters of doctrine, as matters of fact." But I have ſhewn you in a former letter, that you muſt have miſinterpreted the facts which you allege, becauſe your interpretation of them is a moſt glaring contradiction to the doctrine of all God's prophets.

3. Demoniacal poſſeſſions, if your explication of them be juſt, deſtroy the evidence of revelation, or the force of thoſe miracles which were wrought to atteſt it's divine original. If all effects produced in the ſyſtem of nature, contrary to the general laws by which it is governed, or (in other words) to the fixed order of cauſes and effects, are proper miracles; then ſupernatural poſſeſſions certainly come under this denomination. For they ſuppoſe that evil ſpirits inflict bodily diſeaſes, de-

[r] Eſſay, p. 370—376.   [s] Inquiry, p. 198, 199.

prive men of their reafon, render them blind, deaf and dumb, and produce other maniacal and epileptic fymptoms, by their own immediate agency, contrary to the general laws by which the human fyſtem is governed, or to the fixed order of caufes and effects eſtabliſhed in that fyſtem[h]. Now, if evil ſpirits can perform miracles, how ſhall we ſupport the authority of theſe works? How ſhall we vindicate the repre-

[h] It may be objected, that we have not a ſufficient knowledge of the laws by which the human frame is governed, to enable us poſitively to determine, whether poffeffions be contrary to thoſe laws. I freely acknowlege, that had the queſtion concerned any ſecret influence of ſpiritual inviſible agents on the human mind, I could not pronounce ſuch an influence miraculous, becauſe I could not prove that it was contrary to the laws of nature, having no knowlege of thoſe laws by which the world of ſpirits is governed. But the queſtion concerns outward and ſenſible effects, maniacal and epileptic fymptoms, (always included in poffeffions) which were often attended with blindneſs, deafneſs, and other bodily diforders. Now theſe diforders are known to proceed from a bad habit of body, and other natural caufes. And therefore were they to be produced by the ſupernatural agency of demons, ſuperſeding the operation of natural caufes, they would be undoubted miracles.

ſentation

sentation made of them in Scripture, as works appropriate to God; or the use which the Scripture makes of them, as in themselves authentic and decisive evidences of a divine mission[i]? That I may not repeat what was urged in the Essay on this subject[k], I will only add,

4. Your explication of demoniacal possessions casts the greatest reflection upon the character and conduct of Christ and his apostles. I do not mean, that you, Sir, or others in your way of thinking, design

---

[i] Nevertheless, you contend, (Inquiry, p. 189.) that *the working of miracles is ascribed to the spirits of demons*, Rev. xvi. 13, 14. without taking any notice of what was said in the Essay, p. 45, note (ε), and p. 218, to explain this passage. How could you argue from the *literal* sense of this passage, when you call it an *emblematical* representation of what John saw in *a vision?* Inq. p. 188. Recollect your own explication of Rev. xiii. 13, 14. in your Boyle's Lect. v. ii. p. 342.

[k] See Essay, p. 184, and p. 406, concerning the evidence of miracles in general. How much your reasoning discredits the miraculous *infliction* and *cure* of diseases, in particular, is shewn, Essay, p. 403. On the other hand, it has been shewn, Essay, p. 408, that the true explication of the demoniacs of the Gospel, establishes the certainty, and displays the full glory, of the miracles performed upon them.

to afperfe the firft founders of chriftianity. Nothing certainly can be farther from your thoughts. It may, however, deferve to be confidered, how far you may really do, the injury you did not defign. Our Saviour told the unbelieving Jews, *the works that I do in my Father's name, they bear witnefs of me.* Amongft thefe works, he reckons his cafting out demons, to which he refers his moft malicious enemies[1], Herod and the Pharifees, for conviction. Now, if you place this miracle in barely ejecting a fpiritual and invifible being from the human body, and reft even the fact itfelf, his being ejected, upon the teftimony and authority of Chrift, you make him offer his enemies an evidence of his miflion, which in itfelf could carry no conviction, (and which therefore would have been received as an infult;) and you make him urge his authority before he had eftablifhed it, and in order to fupport the proof he gave of it to thofe, by whom it was not acknowledged. According to

[1] Mat. xii. 28. Luke xiii. 32.

your mifreprefentation of him, our Saviour, inftead of faying, with refpect to difpoffeffions, *The works that I do, they bear witnefs of me*, ought to have faid, *I bear witnefs of my works*. But no fuch abfurdity can be fixed on him, who was the wifdom of God, as well as the power of God.

With refpect to the apoftles and evangelifts, confider, I intreat you, in how odious a light you place them. They profefs to give us a hiftory of the great facts upon which chriftianity is founded; and tell us that they were careful to relate only fuch as they were either eye-witneffes of themfelves, or concerning which they had received certain information from others. But I have already fhewn, that you make them atteft facts, which, fuppofing them to be true, could not be known to be fo, unlefs by fupernatural revelation, which the evangelifts did not pretend to. You fink the character and credit of the evangelifts in another view: for you make them refer to a fupernatural agency, thofe maniacal fymptoms which are known to proceed

proceed from natural caufes; and thus to give a fallacious account of the conftitution of nature [m], and fet reafon (our only inftructor in natural things) at variance with revelation. Nor is it merely in thefe views, but in many others, elfewhere taken notice of [n], that your doctrine has expofed chriftianity to contempt; and not only afforded matter of impious mockery to men of a profane difpofition, but (I fpeak it from knowlege) proved a ftumbling block even to ferious and upright minds.

Why fhould you incumber chriftianity with difficulties that do not belong to it? But nothing, it fhould feem, appears to you fo dreadful [o], as admitting two propofitions,

[m] Effay, p. 402.

[n] That your opinion creates a groundlefs dread of demons, and is a fource of thofe cruel fuperftitions, which chriftianity was defigned to abolifh, is fhewn, Effay, p. 399, et feq.

[o] The ground of this dread feems to be, an apprehenfion that denying the power of demons, is the fame thing as denying the power of the devil. But poffeffions do not furnifh any convincing proof of the interpofition of any evil fpirit, (as is fhewn, Effay, p. 386, et feq.) and bear no relation to the devil, who has a different office

positions, which obviate all the difficulties mentioned above, and from which no single inconvenience can arise. One of these propositions, is, that the demons to whom possessions were referred by the ancients, were human spirits; the other is, that by the possessions of demons and their dispossessions, spoken of in the New Testament, we are to understand the symptoms and cure of reputed demoniacs.

The first proposition is established both by the general declarations of the ancients, that *possessing* demons were the souls of the deceased; and by several particular instances of persons said to be possessed by demons, when it appears that those demons were thought to be human spirits. Nor have you, Sir, been able to produce either one

---

office assigned him, that of tempting men to sin. But by your ranking him amongst the demons spoken of in the New Testament, you annihilate his power in this respect: for those demons are nothing in the world. If you would not commit the crime you are pleased to impute to me, *that of laying the devil, and banishing him put of the world*, (Appendix to Inq. p. 332.) you must allow, that he is a spirit distinct from those called demons in Scripture.

general

general declaration, nor even one particular inſtance, to the contrary, from any writer either before, or during, the time of Chriſt, or in the ages immediately ſucceeding it. Nay, after your laboured attempt to diſprove this propoſition, you do, to my apprehenſion, admit its truth, when you ſay [p], that *the larvæ were ſuppoſed to cauſe madneſs*; for the larvæ are expreſsly deſcribed by the Heathens as miſchievous human ſpirits; and they anſwer preciſely to the poſſeſſing demons of the New Teſtament [q].

As to the ſecond propoſition juſt now mentioned, viz. " that the poſſeſſions and diſpoſſeſſions ſpoken of in the New Teſtament are deſcriptions only of the ſymptoms of reputed demoniacs and their cure; it has been ſhewn that they were ſo underſtood in the age of the Goſpel; and proved

[p] Appendix to Inq. p. 313.

[q] See above, p. 38, note (*), and p. 39. It ſhould have been obſerved above, p. 64, note ([f]), that the late biſhop of Rocheſter, in his note on 1 Cor. x. 20. ſhews, that by δαιμόνια there, are not meant *devils*, but *demons*, or the *ghoſts* of deceaſed men.

from

from a variety of confiderations, that they muft be fo underftood in the hiftory of the life of Chrift. It has alfo been fhewn, that the evangelifts by defcribing the diforder and cure of demoniacs in the vulgar language, did not make themfelves anfwerable for the hypothefis on which it is built, and that they have done every thing they could fitly do, to guard againft every fuperftition grounded upon that hypothefis, by eftablifhing the utter inability of demons to do the leaft good or harm to mankind. I muft add, that fhould you be able to overturn the firft of thefe propofitions, that would not affect the fecond. For though the notion of poffeffing demons maintained in the firft propofition, furnifhes one diftinct argument[r] againft the reality of poffeffions; yet independently of that argument, the reafoning under the fecond propofition preferves it's force. In other words, whoever the poffeffing demons of the ancients are fuppofed to be, whether human fpirits or fallen angels, the demoniacal poffeffions and difpoffeffions

---

[r] See above, p. 76, 77.

mentioned

mentioned in the New Teſtament, can not be underſtood in a ſenſe different from that in which they are here explained. One would imagine, that you yourſelf deſpaired of carrying your cauſe by fair argument, and wanted to preclude all reaſoning upon the ſubject, when you reſolve the oppoſition to your opinion into a diabolical agency. The devil anſwers all your purpoſes. Sometimes he confeſſes his own diſpoſſeſſion; and at other times, he perſuades men, *there never were any real poſſeſſions at all**.

I have now examined your ſeveral arguments in ſupport of the reality of demoniacal poſſeſſion, whether contained in your Inquiry; or in the Appendix' to it,

paſſing

---

* Inq. p. 116, & p. 213.

' In caſting my eye over your Appendix, I obſerved the following paſſage, p. 291. " The having familiar ſpirits, implies poſſeſſion, or at leaſt obſeſſion, in the very term." Divination by *ob*, or (as that word is rendered in the Engliſh tranſlation) *a familiar ſpirit*, is a thing very diſtinct from what is called in the Goſpel, being poſſeſſed or vexed with evil ſpirits. I take no notice of the very falſe repreſentation you have made (p. 262.) of the explication I had given of the Hebrew word

paffing over only thofe things that have no immediate relation to this fubject. In the management of your argument, you have taken a very large compafs, and difcovered confiderable ability, and addrefs; and, in my opinion, made as good a defence as the cafe admits[t]. And had not your zeal been

---

word *ob*, which muft appear to every one who will confult Differtation on Miracles, p. 273, and p. 478, where he will alfo find a fufficient anfwer to your argument from it in fupport of real poffeffions. As to the punifhment inflicted upon thofe who practifed divination, it was accounted for, in the fame Differtation, p. 277. Againft whom can your wit be levelled, when you talk of the abfurdity of punifhing any one for the unfavourable make of his body? There is one capital error runs through your whole fyftem of demonology, viz. "You fuppofe that the magic of the Heathens in all it's various branches produced fupernatural effects." But the Scripture, on the other hand, reprefents their magic as founded wholly on human impofture; and all the gods to whom the magicians addreffed themfelves, as utterly impotent and infignificant. Differt. on Mir. ch. iii. fect. 3.

[t] Soon after the publication of the Effay, there appeared an anonymous pamphlet, entitled, *A Differtation on the Demoniacs of the Gofpels*: An advertifement prefixed to it, informs the reader, that it's being printed at that time, was owing to *fome things having lately*

been sometimes too strong for your candour ", your performance would not have been liable to any censure.

We lately been published contrary to the doctrine therein contained. But as this Dissertation is very general, and does not attempt to answer any of the reasonings peculiar to the Essay, and indeed does not contain any thing, but what may be found in your work, and in much earlier publications; I shall take no farther notice of it.

" To the instances of your want of candour taken notice of in my first letter; many others might have been added. I confess, I was totally at a loss to account for your many gross misrepresentations, so much beyond all example, till I found you countenancing the principles of deception, Appendix to Inquiry, p. 275. Though Micaiah said, in express terms, 2 Chron. xviii. 19. *I saw the Lord sitting upon his throne*, you say, *you presume it is not necessary to suppose, that Micaiah had in reality any such vision; for that he himself, in order to undeceive Ahab, if possible, might have contrived this innocent and well-meant fiction.* I do not think that such a fiction (or *falsehood*, for such it would have been, if the prophet had not really had the vision he affirmed he had) can be justified by any goodness of intention. Your maxim would destroy all confidence amongst mankind; and acting upon it in controversial writings, is the ready way to defeat the valuable purposes that might otherwise be answered by them. As to Micaiah's vision, (which was a figurative representation

We are both of us thoroughly perfuaded not only of the truth, but of the importance, of our refpective opinions. It is therefore not only the right, but the duty, of each of us to defend his own. What ground then for refentment can there be on either fide? If writers mean only the advancement of truth, what can tempt them to have recourfe to mifreprefentation and calumny, in order to bear down an opponent? Though truth be more precious than rubies, it is not of equal value with integrity. However laudable it may be to contend earneftly for the faith, our zeal muft not deftroy that charity or benevolence to the whole human kind, which

---

fentation of God's providence in permitting Ahab to be deluded and undone by his own falfe prophets) it was certainly a real one; as appears from the accomplifhment of the prophecy it contained, as well as from the teftimony of Micaiah himfelf. The real injury you have done to the prophet of God, gives juft occafion to retort upon you thofe harfh cenfures (cited above, p. 170, 171.) which you very improperly paffed upon your opponents; but it becomes me rather *to leave you to your own reflections*, as you exprefs yourfelf upon another occafion, Inq. p. 38.

it is one of the greatest offices of faith to promote. Differences of opinion, with respect to matters of doctrine, as well as forms of worship, will always subsist; but they need not produce, and, in well-disposed minds, do not produce, any abatement of affection. I am, with all due respect, and with the sincerest wishes for your happiness,

Reverend Sir,

Your most obedient servant,

HUGH FARMER.

ERRATA.

Page 30, line 5, over epithet put (b).
—— 54, l. 7, from the bottom in the note, dele on.
—— 65, in note (h), and p. 79, note (*), for ibid. read id.—In note (i), p. 65, and in note (p), p. 79, for ib. r. id.
—— 67, l. 3, in the notes, for revertantur r. revertatur—l. 4, for revertatur r. revertantur.
—— 112, note (f), dele Inq.
—— 134, l. 4, for countenance r. authorize.
—— 152, l. 11, for figning r. defigning.
—— 140, l. 7, after the word diforder, add, " When it is faid, that the unclean fpirits crying, (that is, caufing the demoniacs to cry) with a loud voice, *came out*, Act. viii. 7. the meaning is, that the diforder imputed to, or defcribed by, unclean fpirits, left the patients.

The other errors being of little confequence, or eafily difcovered, the candid reader is defired to correct and excufe.

Published by the same Author.

I.

A DISSERTATION on MIRACLES, designed to shew, that they are arguments of a divine interposition, and absolute proofs of the mission and doctrine of a Prophet.

II.

An EXAMINATION of Mr. *Lemoine*'s TREATISE on MIRACLES.

III.

An INQUIRY into the *Nature* and *Design* of CHRIST'S TEMPTATION in the WILDERNESS.—The 3d edition, with additions.

IV.

An ESSAY on the DEMONIACS of the NEW TESTAMENT.

www.ingramcontent.com/pod-product-compliance
Lightning Source LLC
Chambersburg PA
CBHW020758230426
43666CB00007B/747